DISCOVERY

HUNT FOR WITCHES

BAND FOR INDEPENDENCE

TAXATION AND TEA

DECLARATION

REVOLUTIONARY

THIRTEEN

IN GOD WE TRUST

E PLURIBUS UNUM

STARS AND STRIPES

LOUISIANA PURCHASE

GOVERNMENT GUNSLINGERS

OLD IRONSIDES

TRAIL OF TEARS

KING OF THE WILD FRONTIER

UNCIVILIZED WAR

UNDERGROUND RAILROAD

GETTYSBURG

FROM PARIS WITH LOVE

GOLD AND THE WEST

IMPERIALISM

EUROPEAN FIGHTING

CIVIL RIGHTS

NATION WITH GROWING PAINS

A NATION WITH GROWING PAINS

HANK NICELEY

TATE PUBLISHING
AND ENTERPRISES, LLC

Published by Tate Publishing & Enterprises, LLC
127 E. Trade Center Terrace | Mustang, Oklahoma 73064 USA
1.888.361.9473 | www.tatepublishing.com

Tate Publishing is committed to excellence in the publishing industry. The company reflects the philosophy established by the founders, based on Psalm 68:11,

"The Lord gave the word and great was the company of those who published it."

Book design copyright © 2012 by Tate Publishing, LLC. All rights reserved.
Cover design by Nicole McDaniel
Interior design by Ronnel Luspoc

Published in the United States of America
ISBN: 978-1-62024-907-9
1. History / United States / General
2. History / General
12.10.26

Dedication

This book is dedicated in gratitude to all those who worked hard, endured the growing pains, and kept the faith. Some are known, and others are unknown, but all have added their own pieces to the quilt of our nation.

These words were written in loving gratitude to the teachers who did more than they ever realized as they guided young minds in right directions and to loving parents who sacrificed to create a better life for their children.

Mildred Elizabeth Kelley Niceley—Mother
Harvey Tarver Niceley—Father
Reba Dell Keith Niceley—Wife and Teacher

Contents

Introduction
Good Reading and Good Thinking

History is the story of events as they have been filtered through interpretations based on our experiences and values. Events happen as they do. Our understanding of them may change as our experiences and values change.

Our country is a diverse country in geography and population. It cannot be expected that her history will be understood the same way by each citizen. The same event may have radically different meaning to different people. In this book I will attempt to present various events which I have determined to be growing pains for our country. I will include some personal views about their impact on a growing nation. My views are those of a southern Christian, approaching four score years, who loves his country dearly and respects the various cultures which are part of it. You, the reader, may have different life experiences on which to base your judgments and interpretations of these events. As you think on these things, try to get in touch with the reasons for your views. One major reason that America is such a great country is her tolerance of, and respect for, each person's individual worth. I wish you good reading and good thinking.

One Nation under God
by Hank Niceley

Long ago there was a giant
Who thought he could not fall.
He shouted to his enemies,
"I am big and I am strong."
Just try to come against me
And I will bring you down.
But a slingshot and one tiny stone
Put that giant on the ground.

★★★★★

Our power is a gift from God.
Our wealth is from him too.
We are "One Nation, under God,"
Founded in His truth.
A servant is not greater
Than the one he serves today.
Each step away from "under God"
Is a path of peril great.

★★★★★

Our people live in comfort
While many cry their tears.

They look to us to be just
For their stomachs and their fears.
We give of our great riches
And freely share our wealth.
As we look beyond our borders
And reach beyond ourselves.

Hank Niceley

Documents of Liberty and Justice

People came to North America to be free to live and worship in their own way. They fought for such freedom. If they were to become a new and independent nation, they would need some legal structure by which to be governed.

There were thirteen colonies ruled by the British King. The time had come to declare their independence. The Continental congress decided to create a new nation independent from the "Mother Country." A committee led by Thomas Jefferson wrote a document and presented it to the Congress. The Declaration of Independence was signed by the congress on July 4, 1776.

A new nation would need a set of laws by which it would be governed. Discussions were held. Ideas were considered. Agreements were reached. After more than a decade, the guiding document of the new nation was finished. The Constitution of the United States of America was signed by the congress on September 17, 1787.

Many felt the need for specific statements which would guarantee individual rights to citizens of the new nation. James Madison wrote that the people were entitled to certain rights "against any government." He wrote a list of articles. They were edited, altered, and finally signed by congress. All states completed ratification of The Bill of

Rights on December 15, 1791. In later year, several other articles were added to the original ten.

These three documents form the legal basis of a nation, "indivisible, with liberty and justice for all."

Hank Niceley

In God We Trust

In 1864, the currency of the United States was well established in both coinage and paper bills. The country was struggling with the Civil War, which would not end until May of the next year. Abraham Lincoln was president. During the turmoil of this great conflict, an important addition was made to the currency of the nation.

"In God We Trust" was placed on some coins.

The United States was neither finished with its destiny nor with its currency. During the first half of the twentieth century, she had experienced two world wars and the war in Korea. Dwight D. Eisenhower was president (1953-1961). During his term in office, another change was made to the currency of the nation.

In 1955, a law was passed that required the motto "In God We Trust" to be placed on all United States coins and paper currency. It was first put on the one dollar bill, but as new printing plates were made, it was included on the other bills. To some, this has been at odds with the idea of separation of church and state. To others, it is a reflection of the faith and dependence upon God that had brought them safely to the new world and a new nation.

"This is not a Christian Nation!" one said.

"Sure it is. The founding Fathers stated their reliance on God," was the reply. From there, the discussion became more vigorous, each side defending its own viewpoint about the nation and its relationship to the divine.

"God is not the same as Christianity. God is more universally recognized than Christ. Christianity is a religion and our constitution states that government and religion should be kept separate."

"But the constitution says that each person must be granted the right to freely practice his or her religion."

Well, this was a vigorous debate. It was interesting, but it did not change a view or inspire acceptance of the other person's view. When we see the motto, "In God We Trust, where did it come from? How did it get there?

"O Say can you see by the dawn's early light" is the first line from our National Anthem. Most people learn these words, penned by Francis Scott Key, in school. We sing them at public events. They are a part of our national identity. But how many people know the other three verses of the song?

In the last verse Francis Scott Key wrote the following lines.

"Praise the Power that hath made and preserved us as a nation.

Then conquer we must when our cause it is just.

And this be our motto, "In God We Trust."

Although these lines are less familiar, they reveal the importance of God to the emerging nation and its people. We may have differences about the precise relationship between government and the individual, but it seems clear to me that the founders of this country did reveal their "firm reliance" on the divine hand to guide and protect us.

With Roots In God
(Song By Hank Niceley)

(A song included on CD "With Roots In God")

In tiny boats they crossed the ocean
from tyranny on foreign sod.
They gathered here to form a country
where freedom rings in tune with God.
They wrote the words of faith and freedom
"By our creator we're endowed."
Declaring then our firm reliance
on divine providence, they bowed.
America, you are my homeland.
And I am proud to be your son.
Our fathers came to tame a new land.
With roots in God we had begun.
Our fathers sacrificed before us.
Our mothers walked so we could run.
Now it's our time to nurture freedom.
For all our daughters and their sons.
The path we walk into tomorrow
will be the path our children tread.
Let freedom be our destination.
With roots in God, we'll forge ahead.

Hank Niceley

America, you are my homeland
where freedom's bell will ring aloud.
And we all stand within its hearing
with roots in God, on solid ground.
America, you are my homeland
Though torn by some unfriendly wind.
Our standard flies above the storm clouds.
With roots in God we thrive again.

May It Always Be Our Reality

We sing the praises of America because it is our home-land and because it is a wonderful place to live. She has not always been as she is now. She has gone through many growing pains to get here. What she is today is not perfect but it is good. As we sing of her beauty, we are mindful that it is not inevitable that America will last indefinitely. If it is to last will be determined by our vigilance and involvement in her path and our reliance on God to guide us. Our wish for our country is, "May It Always be our Reality".

> " American the Beautiful "
> We sing with civic pride.
> One nation indivisible
> We say as flags wave high.
> We celebrate her birthday
> On July Fourth each year.
> Those who've worn her uniform
> Have fought for freedom here.

★★★★★

> " My Country Tis of Thee "
> " God Bless the USA."
> Do we really hear? Are we sincere,
> As we sing these words today?

If our country really "is of Thee,"
God will bless the USA.
If we use our might for good and right,
America will stay.

★★★★★

" God Bless America"
May we always stand tall.
For decisions great for our nation's fate,
On our maker do we call.
We can still see on our currency
Four words that challenge us.
May it always be our reality
When we say, "In God We Trust."

E Pluribus Unum

When the Europeans came to the new world, people were already living there. The new people to North America began to make a life in the ways of their former lives in other countries. The Native Americans had their own ways. Sometimes these different customs and religious practices complemented one another, and at other times they resulted in conflict.

As time passed, others came from many nations to establish their presence in the new world. North America was a land of immigrants. Many cultures and many religious practices merged to make a new nation. It was not without growing pains that these divergent ways of life and separate purposes came together as one.

Thirteen colonies joined together to form one nation. In 1776, a committee that included Thomas Jefferson, Benjamin Franklin, and John Adams suggested a motto for the Great Seal of the United States of America. These ancient words, "E Pluribus Unum" (one out of many) from Horace's "Epistles" seemed fitting for the nation of immigrants.

In 1873, it was required by law that this motto be placed on one side of every United States coin.

He was the youngest son in a large family. There were eleven siblings. His mother and father had been busy. When everyone was there for the Thanksgiving dinner the table was surrounded by thirteen people. Discussions at the table revealed different opinions on many things. But at the end of the meal they were all family. Blood and love trumped individual opinions.

One day an uninvited visitor barged in and sat at their table. The family was too polite to tell him to leave, so he stayed. The intruder disagreed strongly and loudly with everything that was being discussed. Finally he got up and walked around the table and struck the dad in the face.

The family had been divided at the table on many topics, but when an outsider attacked one of them what do you think they did? Surely, they were instantly united. They had a common cause. They were one.

Our nation started with thirteen units, all individual entities, each with its own personality. They were separated, not unified. The attempt to form a new nation required some measure of cooperation and unity. A national flag was designed and produced. A national purpose was defined. A divine association was stated and put on our coins; "In God We Trust." We had become a family. Out of many we had become one. Woe to he who tried to separate us. This unity was tested many times over the years. The greatest test was probably the Civil War which threatened a permanent separation. Our greatest time of unity was probably

December 7, 1941 when we were attacked by the Japanese forces in Hawaii. This attack solidified our resolve to be "one in purpose" until World War II was over. This same unity of purpose was revealed in a very real way when the Twin Towers in New York were bombed by terrorists. It seemed that all of a sudden we were "of one mind and purpose." E Pluribus Unum ! We would do well to remember such times of unity and resolve to do our best as individuals to continue our motto, "E Pluribus Unum". We are still a nation of immigrants. This is a great part of our strength. A nation of people from different cultures can continue to be our strength or it can divide us. Join efforts of unity. Resist movements of separation. As separate units with separate goals, we will surely fail. As one family respecting our different personalities, and remembering our divine association, we will surely endure.

The Flag of the United States of America

Before 1776, the British Union Jack appeared on the American Flag along with thirteen stripes. After the signing of the Declaration of Independence, this was inappropriate for an independent country. A new American flag with thirteen stars and thirteen stripes was approved by the Continental Congress.

The stars represent the number of states in the Union at any particular time. The stripes represent the number of original states except for a short time when there were fifteen stripes.

1777—thirteen stars and thirteen stripes
1795—fifteen stars and fifteen stripes
1818—twenty stars and thirteen stripes

During the Civil War, President Abraham Lincoln refused to allow the stars of the southern states to be removed from the flag. Stars could easily be added as more states joined the Union. For three months, the Union soldiers fought under a thirty-three-star flag. This was followed by a thirty-four-star flag and then a thirty-five-star flag by the time the war was over.

1908—forty-six stars and thirteen stripes
1912—forty-eight stars and thirteen stripes
1959—forty-nine stars and thirteen stripes
1960—fifty stars and thirteen stripes

The flag of the United States of America has presided over celebrations, funerals, battles, and many other national events. To most citizens, the flag is not just a piece of cloth. It represents the fabric of our way. The American flag has seen its share of our nation's growing pains.

Like midwives, the early settlers went about birthing their dream of a new and different nation. Although these words from the Declaration of Independence, "conceived in liberty and dedicated to the proposition that all men are created equal" had not yet been written, this was their dream. They intended to form a new nation free from the heavy hand of the British monarch. Their cause was important enough to them that they were willing to sacrifice, endure hardships, and even die for the cause. They were fighting Patriots.

They had seen the symbolism of power and its result on the people in their former homeland. The flag represented the king. Flags had always represented monarchs and centralized power and control over the people. The Patriots needed their own symbol to represent the people. They were not professional soldiers dressed in colorful uniforms like the British soldiers who had come across the sea to squelch the Patriots' effort against the rule of the British King. What could they do to unify themselves?

"Honey, I need these curtains to make a flag."

"This shirt could be made into a nice flag that my regiment could follow."

"Our flag will look better than the flag of any other regiment."

The Patriots needed a banner to identify and unify their regiments. Some enterprising Patriots pulled down curtains and used old clothes to make their banners. Each regiment had a different flag. Ships flew whatever flag they wanted. These "liberty flags" unified each regiment but did nothing to unify all of those who were fighting for the same cause.

The Revolutionary War had raged for more than a year before someone created a unifying American Flag. Just who created the first "Stars and Stripes" is a mystery. The making of flags became a going business in New England during those days. Companies provided various supplies to the Patriots. Soon they were replacing the ragtag flags made for individual regiments with crisp new flags.

It is not independently documented that the first American flag was sewed by Betsy Ross, but this tradition has become part of American folklore. She was a Philadelphia woman who had taken over the family upholstering business when her husband died. This is not a direct quote, but according to her family, she told them of her encounter with George Washington and her sewing of the first American flag.

"General George Washington and two Congressional Committee Men named Robert Morris and George Ross came to see me in June of 1776. They brought me a sketch of a flag. They had used a six pointed star on their design. I quickly picked up my scissors and cut out a perfect five pointed star for them to see. I convinced them that it would be better to use the five-point star and went right to work sewing the new flag."

Her nephew wrote this account down. For almost a century, the legend of Betsy Ross and the American flag lay quietly in the obscurity of family memory. Then, in 1870, Betsy's grandson told the story in a speech to the Historical Society of Pennsylvania. The legend took root and grew into the best known story of the beginning of our national flag.

There were many other flag makers during that time. Betsy Ross may or may not have sewed the very first American flag, but her legend is firmly based on fact. The efforts of Betsy Ross and other flag makers helped to unify the Patriots and their cause during the turbulence of the Revolutionary War. They helped birth a new nation. For the first time, a flag represented the people rather than the ruler.

Our national flag has meant many things to many people. To those who followed her into battle, she is a sacred symbol. To those of us who, through the centuries, have enjoyed the blessings of the country she represents, our flag represents our way of life and our commitment to see that it continues for our children. It is not just a piece of cloth. It is a symbol of our way.

Not Just a Piece of Cloth

(A song included in the CD "With Roots In God")

This flag is just a piece of cloth,
Some people dare to say.
But for their right to say it,
Many brave ones had to pay.
For liberty and justice,
A symbol to us all,
This flag's not just a piece of cloth.
May God never let it fall.

★★★★★

This flag's not just a piece of cloth.
Three colors—stars and stripes.
Sometimes for what it's gone through
It's a pretty ragged sight.
It blows in freedom's breezes,
At home and foreign lands.
This flag's not just a piece of cloth,
Made by human hands.

Hank Niceley

★★★★★

The hands that sew the stars and stripes,
In red and white and blue,
Are free to worship God their way,
And disagree with you.
The hands that raise it in the air
Are proud of what it means.
This flag's not just a piece of cloth,
It's a symbol that we're free.

★★★★★

Some followed her to battle
To defeat the enemy
Some fly her high with civic pride
At homes and factories.
Some are folded neatly—
Three corners in a frame.
This flag's not just a piece of cloth.
"Old Glory" is her name.

★★★★★

I pledge allegiance to this flag,
Because of what it means.
Many cried as many died
Protecting you and me.
This flag is what they died for—
A symbol of our land.

This flag is just a piece of cloth,
But it meant much more to them.

★★★★★

This flag's been burned and trampled on,
But she survived it all.
She has seen our bravest heroes
In battle as they fall.
Through all the dark and troubled times,
She still flies high with pride.
This flag's not just a piece of cloth,
For her many died.

★★★★★

This flag has draped the coffin,
As a grieving mother cried.
This flag has bowed her head
When a president has died.
Over long rows of white crosses,
She flies where heroes rest.
This flag's not just a piece of cloth,
She's a symbol of our best.

★★★★★

This flag has shared our sorrows.
This flag has shared our joys,

This flag has flown in windows
Of homes with missing boys.
This flag celebrated with us
On Independence Day.
This flag's not just a piece of cloth.
It's the fabric of "our way."

Hysteria of Fear
and
Ignorance Claimed Its Victims

A witch is a person who is supposed to have supernatural powers. Originally, a witch could be a man or a woman. In ancient times, a witch might not necessarily be evil. First Samuel 28 in the Bible tells how Saul consulted the Witch of Endor for advice before his battle with the Philistines.

The Old Testament reveals that witchcraft is punishable by death. "Do not allow a sorceress to live." Exodus 22:18 NIV

When the people of Ephesus came to believe in Christ as the Son of God, they burned their magical scrolls. "A number who had practiced sorcery brought their scrolls together and burned them publicly. Acts 19:19 NIV

Endor is a city in the territory of Issachar, Jacob's fifth son by Leah. This was fertile land bounded on the east by the Jordan River. Saul sought advice from a witch in Endor. Saul then said to his attendants, "Find me a woman who is a medium, so I may go and inquire of her."

"There is one in Endor," they said. So Saul disguised himself, putting on other clothes, and at night he and two men went to the woman.

Hank Niceley

"Consult a spirit for me," he said, "and bring up for me the one I name."

"Whom shall I bring up for you?"

"Bring up Samuel," he said. I Samuel 28:7 – 11 NIV

The Witch of Endor was either the agent of the devil, or a fake, pretending to have special supernatural insights and powers. Another word for her might be, as used in the NIV translation, "medium", one who communicates between humans and the spirits. Such people were assigned to be stoned to death. "A man or woman who is a medium or spiritist among you must be put to death. You are to stone them; their blood will be on their own heads." Leviticus 20:27 NIV

Witchcraft and sorcery were forbidden. Any supernatural power which is not of God is the enemy of God. It is my opinion that the only plausible explanation for such an encounter is, God allowed it for his own reasons.

She correctly predicted his death.

As time passed, the understanding of the word changed. Men with special powers, good or evil, were called wizards or warlocks. The word *witch* was primarily reserved for women with evil powers. People believed that witches could turn themselves into animals or ride through the air on brooms. They thought some witches married demons and had demonic children. People believed that one could be bewitched. A curse might be put on someone by a witch.

Some magic mixtures were used in witching. Witches could curse animals and crops as well as people.

Witchcraft was practiced in Ancient Egypt and Rome. The early church punished those thought to be witches. It has been estimated that between 1484 and 1782 the church tortured and killed about 300,000 women accused of being witches. This treatment continued in America. There were several ways to determine if someone was a witch. One was thrown into the water. If they floated, they were a witch. If they drowned, they were innocent but dead. Little marks on the skin might indicate places where the devil had touched the person.

The famous Salem, Massachusetts, witch trials began in 1692. Within a year, nineteen people had been hung, and one person was pressed to death. The last witchcraft trial in England was in 1722. The accused woman was set free. Scotland's last witchcraft killing was the same year.

The battle between good and evil has taken some violent turns. Rumors are started. People are afraid. They feel that they must cleanse their town of evil. Many innocents fell victim. The hysteria of fear and ignorance was rampant as it claimed its victims.

Franklin D. Roosevelt said, during a time of war, "The only thing to fear is fear itself." Events such as has just been described are born of fear. When one says they are afraid of the dark, are they really afraid of the dark? The absence of light never hurt anyone. What one imagines to be in the dark can hurt. The people of Salem imagined all sorts of evil things and they chose to believe that certain people were infested with this evil. Whether real witches with evil powers existed is a question to be answered by each person for himself, but fear surely did exist and it caused the people who feared to take defensive actions. Fear was their enemy, not evil powers.

We should be mindful of our fears and try to ascertain their true source rather than transferring that fear to something or someone else. If one shoots at the wrong target, one will never hit the mark. Wrong will be committed and fears will continue.

Salem Was a Little Town

Her People Meant No Harm

Roger Conant came there
In sixteen twenty-six.
To start a brand new settlement,
This place was his pick.
A few miles north of Boston,
With a harbor great and good.
Wealthy seamen built fine homes there
On Chestnut Avenue.

★★★★★

During the sixteen nineties,
A dark cloud settled there.
A servant named Tituba
From West Indies was working there.
She told her tales of Voodoo
To the young girls in the town.
That was the beginning
Of evil's eerie sound.

★★★★★

Salem was a little town.
Her people meant no harm
They thought that they were doing right
As they walked arm in arm.
The stories scared the young girls.
They shook and screamed at night.
When they took them to the doctor,
He said they are bewitched all right.
Cotton Mather was a preacher,
And he aroused the town
To try the girls and cleanse the world
Of the evil they had found.

★★★★★

The trials were held in Salem.
They convicted every one.
It was a year-long witch hunt,
'Till every "witch" was gone.
The Judge was Samuel Sewall
The man that Salem hailed.
Nineteen were hung, one pressed to death,
One hundred fifty were in jail.

★★★★★

Salem was a little town,
But evil staked their streets.
They hung their young on Gallows Hill
But soon they would retreat.

★★★★★

All of them were innocent.
May they rest in peace.
Judge Sewall changed his mind
But five years too late was he.
The years had passed and alas,
All those young lives still were gone.
But Sewall became Chief Justice.
His career and life went on.

★★★★★

Harvard educated preacher
And respected city judge.
Stories told by a servant
And a town in a rush.
They wrote a sad, sad chapter
In Salem's history.
Education and religion
Were as blind as they could be.

★★★★★

Salem was a little town
The Bible they believed,
But education and religion
Were as blind as they could be.

Silent Sounds of Liberty

Let Freedom Ring

Bells have been part of daily life in small towns and large cities around the world. Their familiar sounds have called people to worship or announced the hour or some important event. Bells have been a part of celebrations. They have tolled for the evening curfew and funerals. A bell rings on a fire truck on the way to fight a fire. Teachers used to call the students in with a school bell. Field workers listened for the dinner bell. It is hard to imagine life without bells.

The bell probably originated in Asia as far back as 800 Bc. In ancient Greece, a bell warned people when an enemy was near the city gate. Bells rang for funerals of Roman emperors. Between 550 and 650 AD, bells began to be seen in Europe. Some bells were hung high up in church towers and made to swing so the clapper would strike the bell and make the sound.

As time went on, bells became larger until some weighed many tons. There is a sixty-ton bell in Beijing, China, and an eighty-ton bell in Burma. The King Bell in Russia is said to weigh two hundred tons.

Historical circumstances have given special significance to certain bells. The most famous bell in England is Big Ben—the clock tower of the Houses of Parliament in London. America's most famous bell is the Liberty Bell in Philadelphia.

William Penn was a thirty-seven year old Quaker when he received a grant for a large section of land in North America. He began to govern his province with Quaker-like principles, such as tolerance and equality. On October 28, 1701, he signed the Charter of Privileges which established a governmental framework for his land and people. This document assigned individual rights to the citizens. Freedom of conscience was the predominant freedom which guaranteed freedom of religious practices to all law abiding citizens. Citizens of any religion could hold political office.

Religion was important to many of the founders of America. This is evidenced by phrases such as, "We hold these truths to be self evident, that all men are created equal, that they are endowed by their creator with certain unalienable rights, among these are life, liberty, and the pursuit of happiness," from the Declaration of Independence. Therefore it is not surprising that words from the Holy Bible were inscribed on the Liberty Bell, "Proclaim liberty throughout all the land unto all the inhabitants thereof." Leviticus 25:10 NIV

Hank Niceley

From this starting point many documents of our country that guarantee our freedoms and responsibilities were developed. With the blessings of liberty come the responsibilities of civil society.

It may be good news or bad news, but the ringing of a bell is a means of communication among the people. Bells call people to worship. Bells ring in a new year. Bells toll when a President has died. The clanging of a bell may spread joy or sorrow or anticipation.

The old hymn "My Country 'Tis of Thee" ends with the words, "Let freedom ring." Freedom was a very special thing to those who were trying to establish a new nation based on the idea of "liberty and justice for all." It was a natural symbolism to use a bell to represent liberty. The crisp sound of the new bell rang out across the city until the bell finally cracked. Even though it now sits silently, it is still the symbol of our liberty. It seems to resound even more now with the silent sounds of liberty. Let freedom ring.

The Liberty Bell was made in 1751 to celebrate fifty years of liberties, which had been guaranteed by the Charter of Privileges.

The new country was like a bell ringing to all of the world, "Let freedom ring", communicating our highest ideals of justice and freedom and equality for all citizens. This dream has not yet become perfect, but it is our ideal. We strive toward that goal. We seek to communicate this to all who will listen. We (our country) are the liberty bell.

Many ears listen for its ringing Many eyes watch for its swing. Many dream of the freedoms America affords her citizens. The Liberty Bell in Philadelphia remains a symbol of our intent as a nation. The people are the real liberty bell that rings loud and clear of freedom and justice for all. This means that each of us must respect the freedom of those whose belief and behavior is different from our own. We must respect those whom we do not particularly like. If we are to be a shining light on a hill, we must love liberty enough to want it for everyone . Never forget that the most important word in our pledge of allegiance to the flag of the United States of America is the last word, "… with liberty and justice for all."

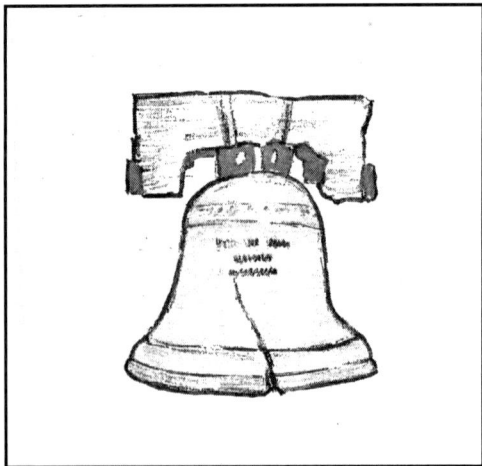

Hank Niceley

Symbol of Our Liberty

The Liberty Bell

They wanted independence
But that was still ahead.
In three quarters of a century,
Freedom's words would be said
But some were making freedom
To worship and to vote.
Some Pennsylvania Quakers
Presented what they wrote.

★★★★★

They wrote a constitution
And gave it a name.
"The Charter of Privileges"
To let their freedom ring.
It separated church and state.
Free to worship or to not.
With voting rights for every man
Who believed in God.
Liberty was growing
Before there was a state.

In a few more years, America
Would let her freedom ring.

*****

Fifty years later
They wanted to celebrate
Their "Charter of Privileges"
It was freedom's happy day.
They built a bell—two thousand pounds
And put it in the town.
It rang for their assemblies
And when court time came around.

*****

It rang there in the State House
Called "Independence Hall"
Until in eighteen thirty-five,
For a funeral it tolled.
It cracked while it was ringing,
And it's still cracked today.
But the "Liberty Bell" has a tale to tell
Sitting quietly on display

*****

Hank Niceley

This symbol of our liberty
Sits quietly today.
But the freedom that it symbolized
Is alive and well today.

They Came for Freedom

Nothing Would Stop Them Now

In the 1620s, a group of English adventurers arrived in the area now called Boston. All but one returned to England. William Blackstone, an English clergyman, built a cabin and lived alone on what is now known as Beacon Hill. A few years later, other settlers moved to the area and named it for Boston, England. Puritan religious beliefs and practices were too strict for Blackstone, so he moved out into the wilderness of Rhode Island.

The Puritans were English Protestants who thought the Protestant Reformation did not go far enough. They advocated more purity of religious doctrine and practice. They purified their religious ways and were disliked by the Anglican Church, the Parliament and the Monarch because of their continual public protests against the Anglican Church. It was made illegal to even attend a Puritan worship service. The powers tried to kill off any opposition to the Church of England by putting a price on their heads.

Some Puritans had gone to other countries, including America. A few were already in Salem when John Winthrop

Hank Niceley

brought a group to the new land in 1630. They formed the Massachusetts Bay Colony where Boston is now located.

Within a century, it rivaled Philadelphia in size and culture. Commerce flourished. Sailing ships came and went at Boston Harbor with cargo from many parts of the world. Shipbuilding became a large industry. Donald McKay built clipper ships in his Boston shipyard in the mid nineteenth century.

Some of the earliest battles of the Revolutionary War were fought here. Bostonians were fiercely independent. They were determined not to pay taxes to England. Having their origins in Britain, they loved their tea. When taxes on tea shipped from Britain got too high, they took matters into their own hands. They had a special surprise tea party on three British ships in the harbor. They threw 340 chests of tea overboard into the water. This led them straight into the Revolutionary War. They came for freedom, and nothing would stop them now.

The Puritans believed that only their form of religion could transform the established Anglican religion. They were the only group seeking an end to poverty. They demanded that all people, even women, be taught to read, particularly so they could read the Bible. Their members were required to work hard to achieve the goals of the church. They had to live exemplary lives to reflect Jesus to others.

They did believe in a kind of freedom of religion, but only for themselves. They made it very clear that people of other faiths were not welcome. They exhibited great anger at anyone of another faith who tried to come into New England.

The Puritans and Quakers had a running battle with each other. The Puritans rejected the Quakers and the Quakers fought back. The Quakers entered Puritan towns screaming and beating on pots and pans. They entered Puritan worship houses during meetings. They ran naked through the town to demonstrate that they must shake off earthly things. The Quakers wanted to destroy the Puritans and vice versa. Neither believed in freedom of religion for the other. It was a recipe for conflict and disaster.

So, all was not friendly and free in the early years of New England. Things seem to have not changed much today. We still experience religious and political hatred and intolerance in a country which was founded on the concept of liberty. Could you welcome, or even tolerate, a mosque in the same block with your church? Could you feel comfortable hearing an atheist expound upon his beliefs? Would a Hindu be welcome in your home for dinner? There are real differences of religious beliefs and traditions in our country. In the past, religious differences have been the cause of much hatred and bloodshed. Can this continue in our country? The answer is, yes. The real question is, "Will we let it happen?" Maybe you and I can make a difference.

Hank Niceley

Boston Loved Her Freedom

Boston Loved Her Tea

They came across the ocean
From the land of their birth.
To worship God in freedom
And make a life of worth.
They built a town called Boston
With harbor filled ships.
But the British troops were stationed there
Against the people's wish.

★★★★★

The citizens of Boston
Loved to drink their tea.
British ships supplied them
But they charged a big tax fee.
The people did not want to pay
Any British tax.
It made them very angry,
So they decided to fight back.

★★★★★

Boston loved her freedom.
Boston loved her tea.
Anyone who interfered
Would be her enemy.

★★★★★

The British shot into the crowd
And three were killed that day.
The citizens of Boston
Would make the British pay.
Captain Preston was the leader
Of the "Boston Massacre."
They tried the man for murder,
But the court did not concur.

★★★★★

Two of Preston's soldiers
Were branded on their hands
And dismissed from the army,
But it did not stop their plan.
The tax on tea was not removed.
That made them madder still.
On Samuel Adams' orders,
They all went down the hill.
Boston loved her freedom.
Boston loved her tea.
Anyone who interfered
Would be her enemy.

★★★★★

Two ships were in the harbor.
Loaded up with British tea.
Unguarded by the British,
They sat there quietly.
Forty or fifty
Of Samuel Adams' men
Dressed to look like Native Americans
Went out for a swim.
They threw the cargo overboard
Out in the harbor deep.
There would be no taxes paid
On all that British tea.
That was in December
Of seventeen seventy-three.
But only two years later
They were fighting to be free.

★★★★★

Boston loved her freedom,
Boston loved her tea.
Anyone who interfered
Would be her enemy.
The "Boston Tea Party"
Threw the king into the bay.
Without a doubt, they threw him out,
Now Boston's free today.

Jefferson's Foresight

Part of the Country's Growing Pains

Thomas Jefferson became President of the United States in 1801. The country was much smaller then. The western boundary was the Mississippi River. Florida was Spanish territory. Most of the area west of the Mississippi River was under Spanish control. Secretary of State James Madison was instructed to make efforts to see to it that these territories would not be transferred to any country other than the United States. His efforts were unsuccessful. In 1801, Napoleon's troops were almost destroyed trying to put down a rebellion in Santo Domingo. The transfer of Louisiana to France did not take place then.

Jefferson saw the danger if France annexed American territory. Congress voted two million dollars to purchase part of the territory. Jefferson was willing to pay almost ten million dollars for Florida and New Orleans.

During the spring and summer of 1803, a treaty was signed. In October, Congress passed laws that authorized loans from Dutch bankers to purchase the Louisiana territory. The purchase was made. The area covered more than 800,000 square miles. It stretched from the Gulf of Mexico

Hank Niceley

to the Canadian border. This essentially doubled the size of the United States. In the following years, boundaries were firmed up and expanded. In 1819, the United States bought Florida from Spain.

It is hard to imagine the map of the United States if other countries had annexed vast parts of the continent. It was a complicated endeavor, but Jefferson's foresight strengthened America. The Louisiana Purchase was a major part of the country's growing pains.

Thomas Jefferson Was President

The Country's Size was Doubled

They declared their Independence
Just a few short years ago.
They had a brand new government.
Now they were on their own.
Population was growing
And moving toward the west.
When they reached the Mississippi,
Other countries owned the rest.

*****

Some were looking forward
And knew that they would grow.
More land would be needed,
But just where could they go.
Florida was Spanish land,
And the land just to the west
Of the mighty Mississippi
Would be a mighty test.

*****

Hank Niceley

Thomas Jefferson was president
And soon he had a plan.
To try to make a treaty
To purchase all that land.
New Orleans was important
And Spain controlled that port.
But soon they transferred ownership
To France, along with more
Now France owned Louisiana
And they held on to it well.
Napoleon was Emperor
And he did not want to sell.
But this military general
Saw the writing on the wall,
When his troops were devastated
In Santa Domingo.

★★★★★

In the springtime and the summer
Eighteen hundred and three,
With a loan from some Dutch bankers.
Congress did agree
To pay almost ten million
Dollars for that land.
That persuaded Napoleon
To sell, and change his plans.

★★★★★

The Louisiana Purchase
From the Gulf of Mexico
To the border with Canada
Allowed America to grow.
Now the country's size had doubled
And New Orleans was their port.
Thomas Jefferson was President
And the country grew once more.

Hank Niceley

A Sure Way to Settle a Dispute

No Second Chances

Dueling has been a means of settling differences between men of high rank for centuries. Disputes over cheating in a game, property, or honor might be the catalyst for one man to challenge another to a duel. It was usually carried out with swords or pistols. Some believed that God would give the victory to the innocent man.

The rules of dueling differed from place to place. The honor of the participants was satisfied with a wound in the French dueling code. In America, death was the rule. The one who had been challenged chose the weapons. In England, swords were most popular. In America, pistols were preferred. A doctor was usually in attendance at a duel.

Queen Elizabeth I of England was first to abolish the practice of dueling. In the 1800s, the United States did the same. In 1801 Tennessee outlawed dueling, and the District of Columbia followed in 1839.

There were many famous duels in the United States. The best known of all happened in 1804 when Aaron Burr wounded Alexander Hamilton with a pistol. In 1806,

Andrew Jackson killed Charles Dickinson with a pistol. James Barron killed Stephen Decatur in 1820. In 1826, Henry Clay fought John Randolf with pistols. This time, no one was hurt.

It is hard to imagine this practice nowadays. Try to visualize the Secretary of State getting into an argument with the Vice President and challenging him to a duel. As they stand back to back in a clearing in the woods, television cameras are trained on them, and a second by second description is being heard by millions of viewers all around the world. One will die.

Dueling was definitely a sure way to settle a dispute. It is now a thing of the past, but the weapons and the outcome have changed. It seems a little more civilized to duke it out in words than with lethal lead. There are times, as evidenced by news releases, that people resort to face to face violence. This is a little different from back to back violence of the duels of the past, but not much. There are what used to be called "rumbles" which test one gang against another. This is depicted in the drama, "The West Side Story". There are very violent man to man professional fights. These may be for profit or to settle a grudge. These are popular for viewers. It seems that many people are willing to pay money to watch two men pound on each other's body until one of them cannot continue. In the old west, there were public gunfights. People watched them from the windows of the saloons and livery stables. People used to gather to watch public hangings. More recently, there have been killings on college and high school campuses. These shooters have usually been mentally and/or emotionally unstable. In almost all cases today, those who kill must face a court of law and appropriate punishment It is no longer socially acceptable for two who have a difference to settle, to go out in the woods and, like a game with formal routine and rules, turn and fire on each other with the intent to kill. It is clear that we have progressed from the duel as a method of settling a difference. In an election year in America we should check our weapons at the door. We are about to have another presidential duel, a debate.

Ambition and Politics

Two Bitter Enemies

One came from the West Indies.
One came from New Jersey.
Both became lawyers
In the sixteenth century.
Both got into politics
And climbed the ladder fast.
They became part of our history
By the shadows that they cast.

★★★★★

Aaron Burr was elected
As a US Senator.
But that was not enough for him.
He always wanted more.
He ran against Thomas Jefferson
For the US president.
The victory went to Jefferson,
And Burr had lost again.

★★★★★

One man reaching for the stars.
One battle he had lost.
But he would try and try again,
But he would pay the cost.

★★★★★

Alexander Hamilton
Opposed Burr in his quest.
But Burr was still ambitious,
So he tried for a little less.
He ran for New York Governor
And thought that he would win.
But he lost face when he lost that race
Opposed by Hamilton again.

★★★★★

Burr issued a challenge
To Hamilton, to fight
A duel with him with pistols—
New Jersey in July.
The year was eighteen hundred four.
The place was Weehawken.
Disaster would come calling
For one of these two men.

★★★★★

Two men reaching for the stars.
Two pistols in their hands.
Ten paces and one moment
Took the life of one of them.

★★★★★

Back to back they stood erect.
Ten paces counted out.
One quick turn and fire returned.
No time to run or doubt.
Two pistols cracking loudly.
One shot hit its mark.
Alexander Hamilton
Was wounded in the heart.

★★★★★

Hamilton died quickly. He had no more time.
Burr was tried for treason
And acquitted for that crime.
He ran away to Europe,
But returned to the USA.
The shot that killed Hamilton
Blew his own career away.

★★★★★

Two men reaching for the stars.
Two bitter enemies.
Ambition and politics,
Would never find their peace.

A Ship and a Poem:

To Save a Piece of History

Oliver Wendell Holmes (1809—1894) was born in Cambridge, Massachusetts. After studying law for a short time, he decided on a career in medicine. After receiving his medical degree from Harvard, he set up a practice as general practitioner in Boston. He taught anatomy at Dartmouth and became Dean of the medical school there.

Holmes's son, Oliver Wendell Holmes Junior, was a famous jurist who served as Justice on the United States Supreme Court for thirty years. When he retired at the age of ninety, he was the oldest Supreme Court Justice in United States history. He is known for his legal writings. Influenced by his service during the civil War, he wrote, "The life of the law has not been logic; it has been experience." In his most highly regarded book of 1881, The Common Law, he stated that the true basis of a legal decision is often "outside the law". This is in line with the previous quote about the life of the law being experience. He died two days before his ninety-fourth birthday in 1935.

Hank Niceley

Holmes always had a love of literature. He wrote essays, novels, and poetry. In 1830, he wrote a poem that became immediately popular. *Old Ironsides* was a protest against the decision to destroy the *USS Constitution*, which is now called *Old Ironsides.*

George Washington had commissioned the building of the *USS Constitution* in 1794. Two thousand trees were used to construct her sturdy oak hull. She was launched in 1797.

She fought in many battles in the War of 1812. In August of that year, she was in a battle with the British ship *HMS Guerriere*. It is said that during battle, someone saw shots bouncing off her strong sides and remarked, "Her sides are made of iron." The Americans won the battle and a new hero *Old Ironsides* was born.

In 1828, the Navy was considering scrapping the ship. The public voiced their opposition to the destruction of this great ship, which bore the name of country's most important document. Oliver Wendell Homes was among those who wanted to save *Old Ironsides.* He quickly wrote a poem called "Old Ironsides," which was published the next day. His poem had much to do with the Navy's decision to restore the ship. A ship and a poem were forever linked to preserve a piece of our history.

"Her deck, once red
With heroes' blood
Where knelt the
Vanquished foe,
When winds were
Hurrying o'er
The flood, and waves
Were white below."
Old Ironsides
Oliver Wendell Holmes

Hoof Beats Faded Away

The Iron Horse Had Won

For many centuries, the horse has been of great service to man. Hunters rode horses as they chased down other animals for food. Warriors rode horses into battle. Horses have been a beast of burden as they carried heavy loads and pulled plows and wagons. They were the best means of transportation on land. The American pioneers depended on horses to pull their covered wagons and stagecoaches westward. Communications depended on the horses of the pony express. Cowboys rode their horses on the long cattle drives. Horses seemed to be irreplaceable.

As a young America growing, there was a need for better transportation and communication. The invention of the steam engine opened the way for a great revolution. The steam locomotive was first seen in American in 1925 at Hoboken, New Jersey. The small engine ran on a circular track. It seemed natural that it be called the "iron horse."

The horse did not go quietly in the face of the new invention. Many thought the steam engine could never outrun the horse. It was inevitable that this would be put to the test. In 1830, people gathered in Baltimore to watch the great race with the new "iron horse."

Peter Cooper had built a tiny steam engine and called it "Tom Thumb" after the famous American midget, Charles Stratton, who went by the professional name of "Tom Thumb." It was so small that he used gun barrels for boiler tubes. The little steam engine stood beside the big stage-coach horse. Then at the sound of the gun, they were off. Neck and neck they ran. Then Cooper built a hotter fire to get a better head of steam. Little by little "Tom Thumb" pulled ahead. Just as victory seemed to be in sight, a belt slipped and the steam engine came to a stop. The horse ran past it and won the race. This victory would not last long, for very soon the "iron horse" would revolutionize America.

In December of 1830, the "Best Friend" began the first regular rail service in America on the South Carolina Railway. When it exploded the next year, the "West Point" took its place. After this, the American railroad rapidly expanded until it finally connected both coasts. On May 20, 1869, westbound and eastbound tracks were joined in a ceremony at Promontory, Utah. A gold spike was driven and America would never be the same.

The horse had finally met its match. Hoof beats faded away as the sound of the nine-pound hammer striking the golden spike rang out across the nation. The "iron horse" had won.

The coming of the railroad was the most important event in the life of a growing nation barely fifty years old. It was the catalyst for an industrial revolution and a cultural revolution in America. Fortunes were made. Lives were changed forever. People were united and people were separated by the new phenomenon.

Travel distances were shortened. One all-day, forty mile long canal trip was reduced to a one hour, seventeen mile trip. The previous long trip from San Francisco to New York was reduced to a few days on the rails. Goods could get to their destination much faster. People could travel more. Dining and club cars were soon filled with ladies in fine dresses and men with top hats. Now they could see, in comfort, for themselves the places they had only heard of.

The railroad made Baltimore competitive with New York in the transport of people and goods to the west. Shares were sold to finance the Baltimore and Ohio (the B&O) Railroad. In less than two weeks they had raised four million dollars. Ruthless rail barons became wealthy.

It was not all "smooth railing" for the growing industry. Opposition was strong from people whose businesses were threatened. Canal and stagecoach companies vigorously opposed the building of rail lines. A few religious leaders said that trains were sacrilegious. The conflict of purposes sometimes turned to violence, but the obvious benefits of the railroad were so overwhelming that even the skeptics were convinced.

It was no easy job to attract workers to lay the tracks. It was hard work and often dangerous. There were many Chinese and Irish immigrant laborers.

Even as the railroad unified the country, it brought change to the lives of Native Americans. As more people went west, their lands in the Great Plains were settled by farmers. Their buffalo were often shot from the passing trains for sport. The herds diminished. Conflict erupted as rail lines crossed their tribal lands. Their lives, like the life of the nation, would never be the same.

Every important movement and development has its pros and cons, its supporters and its opposition. The railroad was, and is, no different. Its benefits are so profound that it was destined to become the most important event in the growth of America. Steam engines gave way to the newer diesel locomotives. New rail lines were built. Bridges and tunnels made it possible for trains to reach more and more places. Even today, in a time of jet aircraft travel, the railroad has a tremendous effect on our entire society. Goods and services are transported to every corner of our vast nation and beyond. Trains are cheaper and faster than roadway traffic. It is fair to say that the railroad continues to be one of America's greatest assets.

The Iron Horse

"Tom Thumb"

She was a tiny engine
Named for a tiny man.
The man was Charles Stratton,
But he had another name.
The tiny engine named for him
Was much smaller than the rest.
"Tom Thumb" is what they called it,
And it proved to be the best.

★★★★★

A man named Peter Cooper,
An ironmaster was he.
He made a locomotive,
As small as it could be.
Gun barrels for her boiler tubes.
He knew that it would find
The speed to beat the horses
Of the local stagecoach line.

★★★★★

They challenged "Tom Thumb" to a race.
He would have to run
Against one of their horses.
Many came to see the fun.
The year was eighteen-thirty
The place was Baltimore.
And as the race got started,
The steam began to pour.

★★★★★

At first the horse and engine
Were running neck to neck.
But Cooper built a hotter fire
And pulled ahead of it.
"Tom Thumb" pulled way out in front.
They thought that he had won.
When a belt slipped and stopped him,
The big horse passed him up.

★★★★★

Other engines came along,
And they outran the horse.
But "Tom Thumb's" race had set the pace
For other engines' roar.
"Best Friend" was the first engine
To pull a US train.
When "Best Friend" blew, "West Point" was new,
So it took her place.

★★★★★

The railroads kept on rolling
Across the USA.
From the Pacific Ocean,
Toward the mid-west plains they came.
Westward tracks continued
Across the prairie land.
Until, in eighteen-sixty nine,
The East and West shook hands.

★★★★★

At Promontory, Utah,
In the mountains near the lake.
A golden spike was driven
To commemorate that day.
When east and west united,
The railroad was complete.
"Tom Thumb" was rewarded,
With victory from defeat.

★★★★★

That little engine did its best,
That stagecoach horse to catch.
In his first race he was second place,
But the horse would meet his match

The race was on. The railroad won
With the "Iron Horse" in the lead,
But "Tom Thumb" was the first to run,
And he lives in history.

Forced onto Reservations

Many Died along the Way

Native American cultures flourished in North America long before the Europeans came. Since they landed on the eastern shores of the continent, the Indian tribes of the eastern woodlands were the first to have contact with the Europeans. For a while, they got along well. The new settlers and the Native Americans even celebrated the harvest together at Thanksgiving. After a while, relations between them deteriorated into small battles. As Europeans moved westward and took the Native Americans' tribal lands for themselves, the battles grew into wars. Treaties were made and broken.

The Europeans tried to get the Native Americans to adopt European ways. The Native Americans did not practice private land ownership. As the Europeans took land for themselves, the Native Americans resisted. Too many the Native Americans were looked upon as savages who must be controlled and dominated. White Americans began their efforts to dominate and control the Native Americans. The White man was determined to remove what they perceived as an impediment to their desired progress. They were successful in their efforts to remove the Native Americans from the woodlands of the East in the "Trail of Tears". Many of the Native Americans were considered to be "savages" and were slaughtered. Promises were made to the Native Americans. Many were broken and have not been kept to this day.

It is fair to say that the results of this success are viewed differently by the White Man and the Native American. It might also be said that the success is not as sure as might be thought at the time. There are still issues of disagreement between the Native Americans and the United States Government.

In 1830, the United States Congress passed the Indian Removal Act. This allowed the government to move all the eastern Native Americans west of the Mississippi River. Most were moved onto reservations in Oklahoma Territory. During the next ten years, seventy thousand were moved from their tribal lands to a new home.

Indian life in America was forever changed. Diseases were introduced to the Native Americans, for which they had no immunity. As they were forcibly moved, tribal customs broke down. Although some Cherokee Native Americans hid out in the mountains to escape the forced marches, many thousands of eastern Native Americans were moved west and forced onto reservations. Many died along the way. One of the saddest chapters of that era was a forced march which the Native Americans call "The Trail of Tears."

This era in the history of our nation is filled with divergent motives. Some are honorable and some are not so honorable. Thomas Jefferson wanted to leave the Native Americans east of the Mississippi and for them to become agricultural people. His motive was to make them economically dependent on trade with white Americans and be willing to trade away their land for goods. In a letter to William H. Harrison in 1803, Jefferson wrote,

"To promote the disposition to exchange lands which they have to spare and we want for necessaries which we have to spare and they want. We shall push our trading uses, and be glad to see the good and influential individuals among them run in debt because we observe that when these debts get beyond what these individuals can pay, they become willing to lop them off by a cession of lands."

This seems to establish that Jefferson's purpose was to make the Native Americans dependent upon the white man's government by seeing to it that their debt got so big that they must trade away their property to the white man's government. Some believe this premise is at work today in America, with an enormous national debt, which continues to rise, Whether this is true is a determination to be made by each person according to his political views.

He continued to describe his view of the use of superior power to crush the weaker people to achieve his purpose.

"As to their fear, we presume that our strength and their weakness is now so visible that we must see that we have only to shut our hand to crush them."

Many plans for the removal of the Native Americans were submitted and rejected for one reason or another, but finally the removal of the "problem" began. The Native Americans were forced to walk from their homeland east of the Mississippi River to their newly assigned home west of the river.

They were forced to leave with little notice or time to prepare. The food given them by the guards along the way was barely enough to keep them alive. There was food along the way to be gathered, but the guards would not let them slow down long enough to get it. Disease spread among them. Infants and elderly died along the way. By the time they reached their destination it was surprising that any had survived.

Prejudice and greed were leaders along the Trail of Tears. In the minds of some this was just a problem to be fixed. The stronger group coveted what the weaker group had. The weaker group was in the way of progress. With well-laid plans, which did not include compassion and respect, they set about to solve their problem. Did their plans work? The Native Americans were removed from the coveted lands but the problem remains. It is visible to anyone who visits a reservation. Speak to a Native American whose ancestors experienced the Trail of Tears and you will likely get a feel for the truth of this disastrous event in our nation's history.

They're Not Like You and Me

The Trail of Tears (A Song by Hank Niceley)

This is a real true story
Of hate, and fear, and greed.
Of people who were different.
This is our history.

★★★★★

There were mountains, streams, and valleys.
There were virgin forests there.
There was fertile land for growing.
There were deer and mountain bear.
This had been their nation.
This had been their home.
This had been their way of life,
But changes were to come.

★★★★★

Some people came from far away,
Across the deep, blue sea.
They were searching for a new life

In a place they could be free.
They built their homes and built their towns
And raised their families.
And soon they wanted much more land,
But how was that to be.

★★★★★

Pain and fear. Trails of tears.
It did not have to be.
Move them out. It's our land now.
They're not like you and me.

★★★★★

The ones they called the Native Americans
Were living on the land
In the eastern mountains,
So the white man made a plan
To move the Native Americans westward
By government decree.
Chickasaw, Creek, and Seminole,
Choctaw and Cherokee.

★★★★★

From the Carolina mountains
And the hills of Tennessee,
They made them all march westward

For many days and weeks.
They took nothing with them
But memories and fears,
As they left their home behind them
And walked the trail of tears.

★★★★★

Pain and fears. Trail of tears.
It did not have to be.
Move them out. It's our land now.
They're not like you and me.

★★★★★

Many died as they all tried
To walk that dusty trail.
If they tried to run from white man's gun,
They knew they would be killed.
It was in the eighteen thirties,
But forever they will hear
The mournful cries of those who died
Along "The Trail of Tears."

★★★★★

Pain and fears. Trail of tears.
It did not have to be.
Move them out. It's our land now.
They're not like you and me.

Unequal Forces

A New Map For The United States

Texas was a part of the New Empire of Mexico. There was a group of Mexicans who had settled in Texas who did not want to be a part of Mexico. The Alamo had been built as a Catholic mission in San Antonio, Texas, in 1817. The Alamo is the word for the many cottonwood trees growing near the mission.

In 1835, Texans decided to break relationships with Mexico. To stop this, General Santa Anna gathered about 5,000 soldiers near the mission. The Texans numbered only about 150 men. The Texans used the Alamo as a fort as they tried to hold off the Mexicans.

On February 23, 1836, the battle began. When the Texans were running out of ammunition, Santa Anna scaled the walls and fought his way into the Alamo. All of the Texans and many Mexicans were killed.

The battle of the Alamo was lost, but it became the catalyst for Texas's independence. "Remember the Alamo" was the rallying cry as Sam Houston pursued Santa Anna. They surprised him during afternoon siesta time at San Jacinto, Texas. The Mexicans were defeated. Santa Anna was captured and forced to sign a treaty giving Texas its independence.

In 1845, Texas became the twenty-eighth state. During the Civil War they seceded and aligned themselves with the Confederacy. It was re-admitted in 1870. The events of the Alamo and just after changed the map of the USA. The Treaty of Guadalupe Hidalgo required that Mexico give vast lands in the southwest, what is now California, New Mexico, Arizona and Texas, to the United States.

The controversy is not over. Some Mexicans believe that these territories belong to Mexico. Carrying Mexican flags, some have demonstrated. But it seems unlikely that the United States map will change anytime soon.

Hank Niceley

A Profitable Business

Invisible Tracks

It seems that it is part of human nature for people to want to subjugate and control other people. Almost as long as people have inhabited the earth there has been slavery. The first slaves were probably captives. Instead of killing their prisoners they made them slaves. After all, what good is a dead prisoner to the captor? A live slave can serve the captor in many ways. Sometimes people were sold into slavery to settle a debt.

Ancient Egypt had captive slaves. They took slaves from Africa to their south and west as well as from Palestine to their east. The Old Testament gives an account of the lives of Jews living in bondage in the Nile Delta in Egypt. Egyptians shaved the heads of slaves so they could be easily identified. Greek slaves could often purchase their freedom with savings from what little money they received from their master. Rome had captive slaves. Some were trained to be gladiators and fight other men and wild animals for the amusement of the Emperor and the crowd.

When one thinks of slavery and Africa, one probably thinks of American slavery before the Civil War, but slavery had existed in Africa long before that. Muslims raided African towns and took black slaves. From the 15th century, Europeans bought slaves in Africa. The booming slave trade was very important to the economy of the African countries. Slave trading posts were established on the Atlantic coast of Africa during the 15th century. The first European customers were the Portugese.

They were quickly followed by the French and the British, Soon the African slave traders were supplying slaves to the colonies in America. By the mid 17th century it has been estimated that one third of the population of the southern states were slaves. They worked in the fields of large plantations. By the 19th century, twelve million slaves had been sold and removed from their homes in Africa.

During the age of enlightenment in the 18th century, a movement to abolish slavery had begun to spread. In 1807, the slave trade was outlawed in Britain.

Abolitionists wanted to do away with slavery. In 1652, Rhode Island passed a law that limited the number of years one can hold a slave to ten years. One person could not sell another person. In 1807, importation of slaves in America was prohibited. The slaves who were already here were not freed until the Civil War half a century later.

During the years before the civil war, a system to help slaves escape to the north was developed. It was called the "underground railroad." It was a semi-organized system to aid runaway slaves with hiding places, transportation, and food. Some have estimated that 50,000 slaves escaped on the underground railway before the civil war.

Harriet "Moses" Tubman was a fugitive slave herself. She was the most prominent activist in the underground railroad. At great risk to herself, she helped thousands of slaves reach freedom. The slave trade was a profitable business to the traders, but the slaves had one of their own to lead them to freedom along the invisible tracks of the underground railroad.

The Abolitionists had a mission. They used any method available to them to achieve their goal. Anti-slavery writings were one of their most important weapons against the evil of slavery. Books, poetry, and all forms of written literature were used to spread the word to counter the idyllic picture of slavery being disseminated by the southern slave owners.

Personal accounts of life in bondage were written. Some slaves, not being able to read, dictated their accounts to others who transcribed it. These narratives were extremely popular. They were translated into several foreign languages. Some former slaves went on speaking tours in the North and in Europe to tell their stories. They told of the pain of family separation and heavy work-loads. There was sexual abuse of black women. They told of floggings and kidnappings. There were also stories of bravery and heroism during daring escapes. These were the voices of slavery's reality.

Probably the most popular of all anti-slavery writings was written by a woman, Harriet Beecher Stowe. In 1852, Harriet Beecher Stowe's novel, *Uncle Tom's Cabin,* became a bestseller. It told the story of Eliza's harried escape from slavery as she was pursued by dogs. This book spurred on the abolitionists' feelings about the evils of slavery. It was first published in serial form. Then, it was published as a book. The first printing sold 5,000 copies in two days. Within one year a half million copies were sold in America and in Europe.

Her book was not so popular in the South. It was called slanderous and false. In Mobile, Alabama a bookseller was run out of town for even selling the book. Stowe herself was threatened and harassed. Once she received a threatening package containing a severed ear from a black person.

Black reaction to her book was generally good, however the character of Uncle Tom has come to have the negative connotation of a submissive black man. Her book's greatest significance is that it outraged the South and ignited the anti-slave sentiment.

The residue of slavery in America still stains the cloak of unity. Although vastly improved, racism is still alive. The old Confederacy is long gone but there are still vestiges of division between the North and the South. It is well to remember that a wrong has officially been righted but scars remain.

The story goes that a single mother who had worked all day, stopped at the store and picked up some hamburgers for dinner. When she got home, her teen daughter yelled at her. "We never have anything good to eat. I hate you." She ran up to her room and slammed the door. Her mother was hurt and sat down on the couch and cried. After a few minutes she decided that this was a good teaching moment. She knocked on her daughter's door and went in. She told her daughter that she had an assignment for her to do. "For one week, I want you to stick a thumb tack into your bulletin board every time you get angry. At the end of the week we'll look at it."

The teen daughter thought that was a strange assignment but she did it. At the end of the week her mother told her to take out all of the thumbtacks. After they were all out, her mother said, "Now look at the bulletin board. What do you see?"

"Holes," replied her daughter.

Her mother said. "Every time you get angry with someone and hurt them is like sticking a thumb tack into them. When you apologize, what remains?"

"The hole," said the daughter.

The mother's lesson was understood. When one hurts another, there can be apologies but the scars of the hurt remain.

America is still in the process of correcting past wrongs. We are still walking the path to: "All men are created equal …" Scars remain. Little hands of black and white may be able to lead us to our destination. Go easy on the thumbtacks and heavy on the apologies and try to heal the scars.

They Call It the Underground Railroad

All Those Who Rode It Were Free

(A song included in the CD "I Have A Dream")

There were no ties, rails, or trestles.
No day cars for first class or coach.
No stations with platforms and people.
No engines with cinders and smoke.

There was no caboose or no brakeman
To switch an invisible track
But it carried many people to freedom.
Its cargo would never go back

★★★★★

There were no long darkened tunnels,
Where long trains can enter and hide.
There were no train whistles blowing,
Their mournful sound through the night.
There was no caboose and no brakemen,

To switch an invisible track.
But it carried many people to freedom
But its cargo would never go back.

★★★★★

They called it the underground railroad,
But it had no train or no track.
Freedom was its destination.
Its cargo would never go back.
It had its own "Moses" to guide it.
A hero to many was she.
They called it the Underground Railroad
And all those who rode it were free.

★★★★★

She grew up a child of hard labor.
She worked in the fields all the time.
One day she escaped from her master
Way back in eighteen forty-nine.
She cooked and she spied and she scouted
For the brave Union soldiers and men.
She helped three hundred to freedom.
They'd never know slavery again.

★★★★★

They called it the underground railroad.

Hank Niceley

But it had no train or no track.
Freedom was its destination.
Its cargo would never go back.
It had its own "Moses" to guide it.
A hero to many was she.
They called it the Underground Railroad,
And all those who rode it were free.

★★★★★

The slaves just called her their "Moses."
'Cause she led her people right out.
Like the Moses who lives in the Bible,
Their Egypt was slavery's south.
They put forty thousand good dollars
As the price on this new "Moses" head
Some wanted to derail her railroad.
Some wanted to see Moses dead.

★★★★★

Her name was Harriet Tubman.
Her mission was freedom for all.
She walked many times in the moonlight
and answered the slaves' mournful call.
Although she was hunted by many,
A fugitive in her own land.
She went nineteen times back to Dixie
To lead them to Freedom again.
They called it the Underground Railroad,

But it had no train or no track.
Freedom was its destination.
Its cargo would never go back.
It had its own "Moses" to guide it.
A hero to many was she.
They called it the Underground Railroad,
And all those who rode it were free.

Hank Niceley

Cast in a Grander Mold

I Have Done My Best for You

He never fought for personal gain. He was tolerant of those with whom he fought as well as those he fought against. His fine character was recognized by the general to whom he finally surrendered. Ulysses S. Grant said of him, "There is not a man in the Confederacy whose influence with the whole people was as great as his."

Robert E. Lee (1807-1870) grew up in a well known family in Virginia. He did not smoke, drink alcohol, or use profanity. He grew into a handsome, energetic man. He was a moral man with a strong sense of duty. He was admired by his fellow students at West Point Military Academy for his brilliance and his devotion to duty. He later was appointed to commander of the academy where he had graduated with honors in 1829. Lee married George Washington's great-granddaughter and raised seven children at Arlington—their home near Washington DC.

It was not an easy decision for Lee to resign from the United States Army and join the cause of the Confederacy. He lived in Virginia when the South seceded from the

Union. His home state had seceded and he could not bring himself to raise arms against his own. He wrote to his sister in 1861, "With all my devotion to the Union and the feeling of loyalty and duty to an American citizen, I have not been able to make up my mind to raise up my hand against my relatives, my children, and my home."

Many families had to make hard decisions during the Civil War. Especially in the border states like my own state of Tennessee, families were often split up because of their stand on slavery and the war. This happened in my own family. My Grandmother fell in love with a man whose sentiments were of "the other side." She was cut off from her family because of this. That scar continued to be present in the family long after the death of that generation of the family.

Lee did not favor secession of the southern states. Neither did he believe in slavery. He had freed all the slaves he inherited long before the Civil War broke out. Lee believed that slavery existed because God willed it so and it would end when God decided. Although he believed the slaves were better off in America than they had been in Africa, he viewed the institution of slavery as evil. One might wonder at the understanding of evil as God's will, but times were different then and people seem to adjust their beliefs and actions as their surroundings dictate.

Lee had spent most of his years in the North and the border states. Until his service in Texas, he had not spent much time south of Virginia. He had not observed slaves up close in the southern cotton fields. He had only encountered slavery at its best and his views were born of his experience. His religious views were also a factor.

A letter from Lee to his wife is included in Douglas Freeman's book *R. E. Lee, A Biography*, which states his views on slavery.

"… In this enlightened age, there are few I believe, but what will acknowledge that slavery as an institution, is a moral and political evil in any Country. It is useless to expatiate on its disadvantages. I think it however a greater evil to the white man than to the black race, and while my feelings are strongly enlisted on behalf of the latter,my sympathies are more strong for the former. The blacks are immeasurably better off here than in Africa, morally, socially, and physically. The painful discipline they are undergoing, is necessary for the instruction of their race, and I hope will prepare and lead them to better things. How long their subjugation may be necessary is known and ordered by a Merciful Providence."

Lee supported the activities of his wife and her mother to free slaves and send them to Liberia. They established a school for slaves in their Arlington, Virginia estate.

He insisted that slaves be enlisted in his army and, for outstanding service, they would be rewarded with manumission and become free men.

Although he believed that slavery was evil, he had no good feelings toward the Abolitionists. He believed their agitation fueled and strengthened the tensions and division between the North and the South. His ultimate goal was not to separate the Confederacy and the Union but to unify them.

It was a hard decision for him to resign from the Union Army and join with the Confederacy.

He led his men into many battles. His famous statement still resounds, "It is well that war is so terrible—we would grow too fond of it." For three days he fought at Gettysburg in July of 1863 where he was finally defeated. His generous nature caused him to take the blame for the defeat instead of blaming it on his men. The next spring, he faced Ulysses S. Grant. Lee held out at Petersburg for nine months before his final retreat. On April 9, 1865, Lee surrendered to Grant. Viscount Garnet Wolseley, a British scholar, summed up the general consensus about Lee, "…A man who was cast in a grander mold and made of different and finer metal than all other men."

These were turbulent times. They were confusing times. Religious views and traditional ways found themselves in vigorous battle on the battlefield and in the hearts and minds of the combatants. Profound personal decisions had to be made. Few totally clear options were available. There were mixed feelings and split loyalties between friends, family and countrymen.

One of the great decisions by both sides in the war was what to do with prisoners of war. Both sides built prisoner of war camps. Prisoners in northern and in southern camps received questionable to terrible treatment from their captors.

The largest camp was Camp Sumter at Andersonville, Georgia. The camp held more than 45,000 Union soldiers during its 13 months existence. There was disease, malnutrition and severe overcrowding. 13,000 people died there. Conditions were so bad there that it prompted Sgt. David Kennedy to write in his diary, "Wud that I was an artist and had the material to paint the camp and all its horrors, or the tongue of some eloquent statesman and had the privilege of expressing my mind to our hon. Rulers at Washington, I should glory to describe this hell on earth where it takes seven of its occupants to make a shadow."

As in all wars, things happen for various reasons that are beyond the control of the leaders. Lee was not responsible directly for the camps such as Camp Sumter but he surely was part of the activity which caused it to happen.

Another great decision that General Lee himself had to make was how to treat the soldiers who had fought with him once the war was over. Lee had just surrendered to Grant. As he rode for the last time along the line of his loyal troops, Lee said. "Men, we have fought through the war together. I have done my best for you. My heart is too full to say more." Lee knew that the young soldiers were needed back home. It was springtime and they would need horses to do the plowing. Grant and Lee allowed them to take their horses home to help with their spring planting. War had not killed the spark of human kindness which, I believe, dwells deep inside of every human being. Sometimes the light of this spark reveals itself at the most unexpected times.

Robert E. Lee was a man of his times who struggled with his own thoughts. He was led by what he thought to be "most true" and best. Slavery was wrong. God was in control. Do your best while God sorts it out. Treat other people, including slaves, with dignity and work for unity. These were his guideposts. Like all of us, Lee had his flaws but history seems to support the proposition that he was a good man.

We Took Our Horses Home

Now Our Horses Are Civilians (A Song by Hank Niceley)

We came from Alabama
To join up with General Lee.
They gave us each a musket
And dry boots for our feet.
A horse to ride to battle
As fast as we could go.
If we did not learn to shoot straight,
We'd be six feet below.

*****

They gave us all some horses
A musket and some boots.
Take care of your horses.
And they'll take good care of you.

*****

We rode North through Tennessee
And we wore the gray with pride.
We saw more than a boy should see.
We were there when many died.
We found him there in Richmond
Fighting for the South.
McClellan's Union army was seven miles from town.

★★★★★

We faced McClellan's soldiers
And sent them in retreat.
Then we rode on to Manassas,
Tired horses, weary feet.
We routed General Pope there
In eighteen sixty -two.
As we rode our horses to the fray
Against the Union troops.

★★★★★

The fighting was bloody.
Both sides lost many lives.
As we rode our horses to battle
Against the other side.

★★★★★

In the fog at Fredericksburg,
The Union men were strong.
Lee led his Confederates
'Till many lives were gone.
We rode on to victory
But a heavy price we paid.
Stonewall Jackson died there, by his own
men was slain.

★★★★★

He led us on to victory
As we followed General Lee,
For three days there at Gettysburg
In eighteen sixty-three.
We fought the Union army
But our fighting men were crushed.
General Lee took all the blame
Instead of blaming us.

★★★★★

The tide had turned against us.
This was our final test.
For nine months there in Petersburg,
We fought Ulysses S.
We had lost a lot of buddies,
But some were still alive.
When General Lee surrendered
In eighteen sixty-five.

*****

They gave us all some horses
A musket and some boots.
Take care of your horses
And they'll take good care of you.

*****

Now the fighting was all over.
The dying was all through.
Back home in Alabama
Spring planting was to do.
We rode them into battle.
We never were alone.
When General Lee said, "They're all yours, boys."
We took our horses home.
Now our horses are civilians
No more battles will they know.
They helped us with spring planting,
Since we took our horses home.

*****

They gave us all some horses,
A musket and some boots.
Take care of your horses
And they'll take good care of you.

TWO WARRIORS, TWO PURPOSES

Custer and Crazy Horse

George Armstrong Custer (1839-1876) was born in Ohio and always wanted to be a soldier. He was always something of "a loose cannon", but his aggressive competence served him well in his Army career. He graduated last in his class at West Point, after which he was commissioned Second Lieutenant.

He fought with the Union Army during the Civil War. His fighting career began at the battle of Bull Run where he carried messages between higher officers. He saw much action at various places during this war. At age 23, he was promoted to Brigadier General. Later he was demoted to his regular rank of Lieutenant Colonel. He played a decisive role at the Battle of Appomattox. He gained a strong reputation during the Civil War.

After the Civil War, Custer was assigned to fight in the Indian Wars. After one of his early Indian skirmishes, he was suspended for a year without pay for being AWOL.

After the Civil War, Custer was assigned to fight in the Indian Wars. He was court-martialed for misconduct following one of his early campaigns against the Plains Native Americans.

He became known as a fearless leader. Some admired him. Others were jealous and said he was a "glory hunter."

In June of 1876, Custer led his men into battle near the Little Bighorn River in Montana territory. It was here that he met his match. Crazy Horse had joined together with Sitting Bull for this battle. When the dust settled, every one of Custer's forces were dead. Thereafter, it was known as "Custer's Last Stand."

In 1946, the Custer Battlefield National Monument was established in southeast Montana. Its more than seven hundred acres include part of the site of his last battle.

Crazy Horse (1844-1877) was the son of a Sioux chief by the same name. Before he was twelve years of age, he had killed a buffalo and had received his own horse. As a young boy he had witnessed the killing of the Indian leader by a soldier at what has come to be known as the Grattan Massacre. Then he saw Indian teepees destroyed by soldiers who occupied a Sioux camp along the Oregon Trail. In another incident, he saw where soldiers had completely wiped out an Indian village, including women, children and warriors. This was enough motivation for him to want to fight the ones who were encroaching on his people's way of life and killing them.

At the age of sixteen he joined a war party and quickly established his reputation for bravery as he rode out in front of the others. As he was riding close to one of the best warriors, the warrior's horse was shot out from under him. He fell to the ground and was being surrounded by soldiers who would surely kill him. Crazy Horse jumped down from his horse and helped his wounded Indian brother up into his saddle, jumped on behind him and road off carrying him to safety.

At age eighteen, his father gave his son his name, Crazy Horse because of his bravery. Young Crazy horse was already becoming something of a legend among his people. Sitting Bull gave Crazy Horse one of the highest honors a young man could receive, the title of "shirtwearer".

When he grew into manhood and became known as a fearless fighter for his people, the Minneconjou band of Oglala Sioux, his father gave him his name.

The US government had ordered him to go to a reservation. When he would not go, the US cavalry destroyed his village. Motivated by revenge, he fought everywhere he could and always won.

1876 was an eventful year. The time had come for the two fighters to face each other . The place was Little Bighorn. Eight days after defeating General George Crook at Rosebud, Montana, Crazy Horse led the Sioux against General Custer at Little Bighorn. Custer and all of his men were killed. Crazy Horse eventually surrendered and was killed by a soldier at Fort Robinson in Nebraska in 1877.

Each of these young warriors died before reaching forty years of age. They are remembered in different ways by different people. When he was told where and how to live by the ones who had destroyed his village and killed his people, he would not go.

Self defense is a basic human instinct. If one's way of life and property is being threatened, one has only a few choices. One can give in and do what you're told, one can move on to another place, or one can fight for his people and his honor. Crazy Horse put it all on the line. He risked his own life and safety to fight for his people. He was cunning and brave and almost always won.

If a man is not willing to fight for his family and friends, what will he risk everything for? The bravery of Crazy Horse shines in stark contrast to the ruthlessness delivered by some of the Army troops. Each side probably thought they were in the right. But the question is, how does one settle differences with others who share the same territory? Who, in this case, was taking land from the other by force? Who was defending their traditional way of life and their long-occupied territory? Right is not always clear in every situation, but defenders and aggressors played their own roles in this turbulent era. We, their followers, must decide the merits of each for ourselves in the light of what has happened since then- an insight they did not have.

Custer and Crazy Horse were both warriors for their separate causes. They are both burned into the pages of our nation's history. Each has left his legacy. Each is remembered for Little Bighorn. They are both gone now but in the hearts and minds of their people they live. There is a monument for "Custer's Last Stand" at Little Bighorn. There is a huge monument cut into a mountain in the Black Hills of South Dakota for Crazy Horse. Still, His memory will not go. To his people, Crazy Horse is still alive.

The natural way of life of North America's first inhabitants was forever altered by the invading white man. They will never again see the days of their way of living with the land. Europeans had other plans for the land and war was one of their methods to eradicate their problem. To the Native Americans, these times meant defeat and subjugation. To the white man, it meant victory, at least as defined by their own aspirations. The nature of the country which emerged from the Civil War/Indian Wars era is a mixture of good and bad, depending who is reviewing it. Today, Native Americans and Invading Americans coexist in a tenuous relationship. Can we justify past atrocities by the resulting industrial progress? How will successive generations view the actions of their ancestors? One group got to choose where the other group would live. The other group had to live where they were told. If one is optimistic, one can envision a future of harmony and respect despite past mistakes by both parties.

Crazy Horse Is Still Alive

In Their Hearts and on That Mountain
(A Song by Hank Niceley)

As a boy they called him "Curly."
His skin and hair was light.
He was a brave young warrior,
But the lad was always quiet.
The Sioux called him "The Strange One"
For he had some special powers.
He led the fights for his people's rights.
He was never called a coward.

★★★★★

One day he got the order
From the US Government.
"Go to a reservation,"
But he disregarded it.
He led the Cheyenne and the Sioux,
As the victory they took.
At Rosebud, in Montana
They defeated General Cook.

★★★★★

Crazy Horse was young and brave.
He fought for freedom, too.
He was their greatest hero,
Just fighting for the Sioux.
He fought them everywhere he could
And beat them every time.
But he would not be satisfied
'Till he won or 'till he died.

★★★★★

When he won his first battle,
His father was the chief.
He gave his name to "Curly"
Who had never known defeat.
He fought them for his way of life
And never had remorse.
Now everybody knows his name—
That Sioux named Crazy Horse.

★★★★★

His battles were not over,
With the ones who took his land.
It was only eight days later
That he fought them once again.
Little Big Horn was the battle place.

General Custer was the man.
He wiped out Custer's soldiers.
That was Custer's last stand.

*****

Crazy Horse was young and brave.
He fought for freedom, too.
He was their greatest hero
Just fighting for the Sioux.
His life was taken from him.
But he will never die.
In the hearts of his own people,
He will always be alive.

*****

Some of the Sioux were jealous,
And friends with the white men.
So Crazy Horse surrendered,
And they arrested him.
As a soldier forced him in a cell
He killed Crazy Horse.
Now Crazy Horse will never fight
For freedom anymore.

*****

Crazy Horse was young and brave.

He fought for freedom, too.
He was their greatest hero
As he fought for the Sioux.
His life was taken from him,
But he will never die.
In the hearts of his own people,
Crazy Horse is still alive.

★★★★★

In the Black Hills of Dakota
On a mountain way up high,
Crazy Horse still rides in freedom
Underneath his nation's skies.
They took his freedom and his life,
But he will never die.
In their hearts and on that mountain,
Crazy Horse is still alive.

A Time of Friendship

A Common Love of Liberty

It is a friendly gesture to give and to receive gifts. Some gifts will not last. Some friendships do not last. Some gifts stand as a permanent testimony to a time of friendship and common purpose. This friendship was between two countries. The common purpose was liberty.

It was suggested that France build a monument that symbolized liberty. The idea caught on, and the project was begun in Paris. Frederic Auguste Bartholdi, a sculptor, began building models for the statue. The size grew and grew until it was too large to fit into any studio in Paris. Finally, it was constructed outside in the street. The final project was so large that an expert in iron structure was engaged to build the framework for the huge statue. Gustave Eiffel, of Eiffel Tower fame, designed the strong interior framework. The frame is made of iron, and the statue is made of sheets of copper. It was a costly endeavor, so funds were collected from small gifts from the French people.

America was celebrating one hundred years of independence. France wanted to give the young country a gift for the occasion. Bartholdi had chosen an island in the New York harbor as the site for his huge statue. It would require a fitting base. The money to build the base on Bedloe's Island was raised from gifts from the American people.

This great gift of friendship and love of liberty was shipped across the Atlantic Ocean in sections and reassembled on the land, now known as Liberty Island. On October 18, 1866, President Grover Cleveland dedicated the big statue with French and American dignitaries in attendance.

The Lady of Liberty stands among the broken chains of tyranny as she holds high the torch of freedom. In her left hand is a law book inscribed with July 4, 1776—the date of United States independence. The entire statue and pedestal rise about three hundred feet above the waters of the harbor.

A small replica of the Statue of Liberty was sent to France. It now stands on a bridge over the Seine River in Paris. Friendship and common purpose gave the world one of its most recognizable and loved monuments.

Emma Lazarus' poem, "The New Colossus" was inscribed on the pedestal in 1903. Some of her words are:

Mother of exiles, from her beacon-hand
Glows world-wide welcome;
"Give me your tired, your poor,
Your huddled masses yearning to breathe free,
The wretched refuse of your teeming shore,

Send these, the homeless, tempest-tost to me."

The most obvious meaning of the Statue of Liberty is political cooperation and friendship between France and the United States of America. But there is more to the story. The history of this statue is a history of diversity and change. While the statue was crossing the Atlantic the two countries could not agree on a general trade arrangement. There was a tariff war. France placed a ban on importation of American pork. The United States retaliated with its own restrictive measures. Some might view the statue as a peace offering in 1886, in the midst of this era.

There is some evidence that some related the statue on the abolition of slavery in America. "The Cleveland Gazette", an African American paper, published this editorial which reveals such a viewpoint. "It is proper that the torch of the Bartholdi statue should not be lighted until this country becomes a free one in reality. 'Liberty enlightening the world' indeed! That expression makes me sick. ..."

At the time of World War I the statue was used prominently in advertisements for Liberty Bonds in order to promote loyalty of immigrants to the Allied cause in the war. The statue has been associated with immigrants since its beginning. In 1972, a new museum of immigration was opened at the base of the statue. In 1965, President Lyndon Johnson signed an important change in immigration law in front of the Statue of Liberty.

Political meaning of the statue has been assigned to the statue by people outside the United Stated and France. In 1889 Chinese students erected an image of the statue in Tiannamen Square. It was referred to as the "Goddess of Democracy." The lady of Liberty led them in an unsuccessful effort for change in their own country.

The Statue of Liberty had found its place in popular culture. It has been used in countless advertisements for all sorts of products and causes. It has appeared in the popular art of Peter Max and the art of other artists.

Michael Jackson included an image of "The Lady of Liberty" in his popular video, "Black and White", representing contemporary American race relations.

So, change has marked her life. What might seem to be a simple gift of friendship from one country to another has become much more through the years. Images have power. Bartholdi never envisioned such a variety of interpretations of the statue but it has meant many things to many people. What does it mean to you?

Both Countries Loved Their Freedom: Lady Liberty

Nickels, dimes, and centimes,
Dollars and francs.
Collected from the people
Of America and France.
To buy a birthday present
To sail across the sea,
To celebrate one hundred years
Of America's liberty.

★★★★★

A sculptor named Bartoldi
Built a statue so big
He had to build it in the street,
And that's just what he did.
The people watched him make it
And heard his hammer sound,
As he shaped the copper pieces
In Paris, pound by pound.

★★★★★

He got a man named Eiffel
To build the frame inside,
Strong enough to hold it,
So he built the frame of iron.
When the statue was all finished,
They put it on a ship,
But it had to go in pieces
Because it was so big.

★★★★★

Its new home was an island.
A pedestal was there,
One hundred fifty feet tall,
In the New York harbor air.
When the pieces were assembled,
The statue was complete.
From the burning torch to the ground
Was about three hundred feet.

★★★★★

A gift from France to America
To help them celebrate
One hundred years of freedom
In the United States.
A smaller replica was sent

From America to France.
Two gestures of friendship
Two countries shaking hands.

★★★★★

Both countries loved their freedom
Both had fought for liberty.
She still stands in New York harbor
For you and me to see.
With burning torch of freedom
And broken chains of tyranny,
She's known throughout the world
As Lady Liberty.

What Would Be Her Purpose

Imperial Power?

In the early1800s, large parts of North American were controlled by Spain. The Louisiana territory was transferred to France and bought by the United States in 1803. Florida was purchased in 1819. After the Civil War, interest in expansion died down for a while.

In the 1870s and again in the 1890s, fighting engulfed the island of Cuba. It seemed that it would continue forever. Neither Spain nor the Cubans could get the upper hand for long. Some American newspapers reported, in exaggeration, that one fourth of all the people in Cuba had been killed. Under American pressure from President McKinley, Spain gave limited self rule to Cuba within the Spanish empire. Cuba would have no part of it. She wanted complete independence.

Cuban rebels continued the fighting and the rioting in Havana. The United States warship *Maine* was sent to protect the American citizens there from the rioters. On January 15, 1898, she arrived in the harbor. On February

Hank Niceley

15, the ship was destroyed by an explosion. About 250 people on board were killed.

The United States declared the independence of Cuba and stated that it was not their intentions to annex the island. On April 25, 1898, the United States declared war against Spain. The first battle was in the Philippines. George Dewey achieved a decisive victory there on May 1, 1898. On June 22, US troops landed on Cuba. Both white and black soldiers fought side by side. The invasion of Puerto Rico followed, and in July, Manila was occupied.

On December 20, 1898, Cuba was given independence from Spain. The Philippines and Guam were given to the United States. The United States paid 20 million dollars for some property in the Philippines.

A growing nation struggled with an important question that year. What started as an attempt to liberate the people of a small island quickly spread into a world-wide conflict. The Spanish American War brought America face to face with the question, "Do we really want to be an imperial nation?" If one reviews the history of the United States for the next century, one might come to one of two conclusions, or maybe a little of both. (1.) The United States wanted to be the leading military and economic power in the world and pursued that goal with all vigor. (2.) The United States was caught in circumstances which forced it to become involved in foreign conflicts for their own security and that of their friends. Whatever the reason, the United States has been continually involved in armed conflict around the world.

The Spanish-American War was short and decisive. The U.S. Navy showed overwhelming force against the feeble Spanish fleet. It resulted in the freeing of Cuba. The peace treaty gave Guam, Puerto Rico and the Philippines to the United States. Along with the voluntary joining of Hawaii, this gave the United States a major Pacific presence. The leasing of Guantanamo Bay in Cuba for a Naval Base added to our capacity to guard the Panama Canal and our Gulf coast.

After defeat of Spanish forces in Manilla and ceding of the Philippines to the United States, fighting broke out with Philippine revolutionaries. The revolutionaries were defeated but 20,000 rebels and about 1,000 Americans lost their lives.

In April of 1914, in what is known as the "Tampico Affair", some American sailors were arrested by the Mexicans. President Woodrow Wilson sent United States troops to occupy the Mexican city of Veracruz for six months. In 1916, Poncho Villa crossed into New Mexico with 500 Mexican soldiers to rob banks to support his troops. General John J. Pershing chased them back into Mexico and secured the Southern border in 1917.

By the Summer of 1918, General Pershing was in Europe in command of one million United States "doughboys" with 25,000 coming every month. This war ended with the signing of an armistice by Germany in 1918.

During the 1920s efforts were made to decrease armaments of the leading world powers. The number of warships was reduced which helped to avoid further conflict in the Pacific. This lasted only ten years. The treaties were not renewed and tensions began to escalate into the 1930s.

World War II raged for six years and involved almost every part of the world. The United States has been supplying war materials to the British, The Soviet Union, and the Republic of China. Following the Japanese attack at Pearl Harbor in Hawaii in 1941, the United States was officially a combatant in the war. Germany and Italy declared war on the United States and a global conflict was on. 2,000 airmen and sailors had been lost at Pearl Harbor. Names like Midway, Iwo Jima, and Okinawa became household words in America. Major fighting was occurring in Europe, North Africa and the Pacific. Then came the atomic bombing of two Japanese cities followed by the Japanese surrender. When Germany surrendered in 1945, the Great War was over.

The United States was now a super power. During the next decades, she supplied military supplies and other involvement in military actions against the Soviet Union. Nuclear weapons were now a part of the superpower arsenals. This did not deter or ever slow the armed conflicts.

The Korean War lasted about three years and involved many nations and the United Nations. This war took many lives and did not settle anything. Korea remains a divided country at the 38th Parallel.

United States's involvement in armed conflicts continued. There was Lebanon in 1958, the Dominican Republic in 1965, and Vietnam, which lasted from about 1955 to 1975. Much American blood and treasure was lost in Viet Nam and dissention and violence stalked our streets at home because of the war.

In 1973 the draft ended leading to an all volunteer military. Military involvement continued with the Tehran rescue fiasco, Grenada and Beirut in 1983, Libya, Panama the Persian Gulf War in 1990 and 1991, Somalia, Haiti, Yugoslavia, Iraq, and Afghanistan.

From a review such as this, one might get the idea that warfare is a way of life for the United States. This assumption would be correct. The real question is why. Is this a way of life which has been thrust upon us because of circumstances not of our making? Is our continual involvement out of a spirit of help for our friends? Or do we simply thrive on conflict and warfare and desire winning? Motivation for our way of life is probably a mix of all of these with different amounts of each at different times. One wonders what the outcome would have been for lives which were lost in these conflicts if they had been lived out. This is not to say that all of these lives were lost for nothing. On the contrary, their sacrifice has provided freedom for millions. That is a worthy purpose. Someone has said that "War is Hell". Those who have experienced it first hand and close up would probably agree. War is also a fact of life. We must all weigh its benefits and its losses for ourselves and as a nation. I pray that those who have power to initiate violent action in our names will have divine guidance as they make great decisions.

Great Debates and Growing Pains

What Will She Become

The Civil War divided her
But healing was to come.
One nation indivisible
With better things to come
Some years of reconstruction
And building unity.
Thoughts of more expansion,
Not what they used to be.

★★★★★

Then her battleship exploded
One January day,
In the harbor at Havana
In eighteen ninety-eight.
Two hundred people died there
On the "Maine" that day,
And plans for freeing Cuba
Were quickly underway.

★★★★★

War was declared one April day
Against the Spanish power.
The battle for the Philippines
Was the first one in that war.
Before the year was over
Cuba would be free,
And Guam and Puerto Rico
Would be US property.

★★★★★

One fighter became famous
As he charged up San Juan Hill.
He became the president,
Teddy Roosevelt.
But the nation was still growing,
And some thought she should keep
All the places we had fought for.
Others wanted only peace.

★★★★★

America had to answer
This question for herself.
Did she want to build an empire,
Or give up what she held?
The answer was important
To the nation's future plans.

Would she be freedom's champion
Or take all that she can.

★★★★★

The history books refer to it
As the Spanish-American War.
But American was fighting
Spain and something more.
Through great debates and growing pains
What would she become—
Imperial oppressor,
Or freedom's champion?

Gold for Sale

Two Cents an Acre

It is doubtful if Secretary of State William H. Seward realized the value of his deal when he negotiated a treaty with Russia to purchase Alaska. The treaty was pushed through the United States Congress and signed by President Andrew Johnson on June 30, 1867. By this agreement the United States had bought Alaska for about two cents an acre. The total purchase price was $7,200,000.

The Russian flag was replaced with the thirty-seven-star United States flag at Sitka on October 18, 1867. Some Russian residents decided to stay on. By the terms of the treaty, they became American citizens. Many people thought that Alaska was nothing but a frozen wasteland. They referred to this purchase as "Seward's Folly" and "Seward's Ice Box." Seward had not seen Alaska at the time of the purchase, but he visited southeast Alaska two years later in 1869.

Gold was being discovered in various parts of Alaska during the last part of the seventeenth century. In the last decade of the century, thousands of hopeful prospectors came to try their luck in the gold fields. They had heard stories of gold for the taking, and they wanted to get their share.

The Alaskan gateway was Skagway. From there they went on through the mountain pass to Whitehorse and on into the Yukon as they chased their golden dreams. Since they were all competing for the same gold, there were many fights and arguments along the way as each one tried to get there first. Some found gold and became wealthy, but most of them were disappointed in their quest. Life was hard there. There was gold for the taking, but they soon learned that the taking would be tough.

Dawson City was a rough town. It was the center of the great gold rush along Bonanza Creek. The scene in the spring when the ice on Bennet Lake began to break, has been described as a mob of several thousand rough hopefuls. They put their home made boats into the water to go north to the Yukon to find their fortune. Most of them did not make it. The river and the cold were formidable enemies. In one popular tavern in Dawson, there was a tradition of drinking from a mug which held a human toe. Stories about the origin of such a tradition vary but it is still practiced there by tourists who visit the Red Dog Saloon.

Many dreams were born there. Many dreams died there. The romance and adventure of Alaska are one of America's greatest treasures. Treasures are to be protected and preserved.

"Seward's Folly" turned out to be one of the best bargains ever purchased. There were millions of acres of beautiful land. I wonder if they would have called it "Seward's Folly" if Russia had put a sign in Alaska that said, "Gold for Sale, Two Cents an Acre." This purchase should be called "Seward's Foresight". This land that we call Alaska has proved to be an invaluable asset to the United States. There is no doubt that things would be different if Alaska had remained a part of Russia. Our participation during the cold war era would have been much closer to home. The economic treasure of Alaska has yet to be tapped. During summertime, huge cabbages and other vegetables grow as big as bushel baskets. There is much oil to be taken in Alaska. The tourist business is huge there during summer months. Alaska is a refueling stop for civilian and military flights to and from the Far East. Fishing in Alaska supplies food for tables all around the world. These are just a few of the benefits of "Seward's Foresight." But one of the greatest, for one who has been fortunate enough to experience Alaska several times, is its natural beauty. The vastness and variety are unparalleled. There is much more to be discovered in Alaska. May we who live today be wise enough to preserve this "Last Frontier" for future generations.

Gold for the Taking

But the Taking Would be Tough
(A Song by Hank Niceley)

We heard of golden rivers
In the tundra way up north.
Alaska and the Yukon,
Were fortune's open door
We dreamed of wealth and thought that
Our dreams would be enough.
Gold for the taking—
But the taking would be tough.

★★★★★

We started out from Washington in 1898,
Going north to Alaska
For fortune and for fame.
When we got into Skagway,
The town was going strong.
With Soapy Smith and all his gang ,
But we did not stay there long.

✶✶✶✶✶

Gold for the taking—
But the taking would be tough.

✶✶✶✶✶

We got ourselves some horses
And headed north one day.
You'll never get them through
Dead-Man's pass, they say.
We made it on through Whitehorse.
The wind was icy cold.
We waited for the ice to break
And dreamed of glittering gold.

✶✶✶✶✶

Ten thousand grubby hopefuls
Were camped there by the lake.
You should have seen the scramble
When the ice did finally break.
There were seven thousand boats
In the icy waters there.
Everyone determined
To be first to get his share.

✶✶✶✶✶

Gold for the taking—
But the taking would be tough.

★★★★★

We floated down the Yukon
To try to stake our claim
When we got to the gold fields,
We found we were too late.
Others there before us
Had staked out all the claims.
There were many killed in anger
Looking for someone to blame.

★★★★★

Gold was for the taking
Were the stories that we heard.
But many froze to death
When the bitter truth they learned
Buckets full of nuggets
Filled every hopeful's mind.
But they never ever dreamed of
The hard luck they would find.

★★★★★

We dreamed of golden rivers
In the Yukon way up north.

★★★★★

Gold for the taking—
But the taking would be tough.

Nome

Canine Heroes in the Arctic

In 1898, gold was discovered on Anvil Creek and Snow Gulch at Nome, Alaska. Before long, this little town on the Bering Sea was completely inundated with forty thousand hopeful miners. They established a tent city there seven hundred miles west of Fairbanks. When the gold rush was over, Nome went back to a small Eskimo town. Being isolated with only one doctor, they did not have the needed medicine.

Dog sleds have long been used in arctic areas for transportation. In these snowy regions, it is often the only way to transport supplies, especially in the winter months. A hearty dog named "Husky" is a popular breed for dog sleds. Dog teams are seven to ten dogs. The lead dog is out front as the others follow him. Their driver gives orders to the lead dog.

The best of these huskies could go incredible distances and pull heavy loads through the ice and snow. They were the life-line for many of the small settlements in the arctic regions.

In 1925, diphtheria was discovered in two of the children of Nome. The needed medicine was eight hundred miles from them. A heroic effort by sled dogs led by the lead dog, Balto, delivered the medicine from Anchorage just in time to save the town of Nome. The modern dogsled race, known as the Iditarod, commemorates their eight hundred-mile journey.

American people are resourceful, especially those who have chosen to live their lives in the sometimes harsh northland of Alaska. When we face hardships of any kind, we have always found a way to overcome them. When someone is in need, we are givers. This story is a microcosm of the spirit of America. People, and even their trained animals, have "the right stuff" and are willing to suffer themselves to aid others. The people of Anchorage and their dogs could have chosen to be sorrowful for the people of Nome and stay in their own safe place, but they chose to risk their own lives and give up their comforts to save the people who needed help. This is the story of heroes, both human and canine. Twenty hours through some of the most threatening territory and weather was a growing pain for the individuals involved, human and canine. It was also a growing pain for good for America. The spirit triumphed over the body and the result was an extension of the best in us. This is the American spirit.

Hank Niceley

Balto the Hero

He'll be Forever Known
(A song by Hank Niceley)

This is the real true story
Of the bravest dog alive.
He lived in Alaska
In 1925.
The smartest and the strongest
Lead dog on the trail
He looked ahead and pulled the sled
As he wagged his husky tail.

★★★★★

His driver's name was Gunnar.
He loved his sled dogs all.
He knew that they were ready
Anytime their driver called.
They'd follow Balto anywhere
That Gunnar said to go.
Through the snow and ice and howling wind,
No stopping did they know.

★★★★★

Balto the hero.
Lived in the ice and snow.
There was nowhere in the frozen north
That Balto could not go.
The bravest and the fastest,
He'll be forever known
As the dog who saved the people
Who lived way up in Nome.

★★★★★

The night had been a long one
In the little cabin home
Two children getting sicker
As the winter winds did blow.
There was just one doctor in the town
So the parents called him up.
He checked them out, there was no doubt.
They had diphtheria.

★★★★★

Without some special medicine
The children soon would die.
And all the others in the town
Would be sick with fevers high.
The doctor had to find a way
And he had to find it fast.

For the medicine to get to Nome,
Or the people would not last.

★★★★★

The doctors down in Anchorage
Put it on a train to go
Eight hundred miles, but in a little while
It got stuck in the snow.
They were seven hundred miles away,
So now what could they do?
Dogs who knew the way could do
What that train could not do.

★★★★★

Balto the hero.
Lived in the ice and snow.
There was nowhere in the frozen north
That Balto could not go.
The bravest and the fastest,
He'll be forever known
As the dog who saved the people
Who lived way up in Nome.

★★★★★

Through the January snow and
ice the race for Nome began.

Twenty-one teams took their turns.
With the medicine they ran.
The medicine was wrapped in fur
So it would not freeze.
When one dog died, the driver tied
Himself up with the team.

★★★★★

Balto and his driver were
Waiting for their turn
From Bluff to Point Safety
Was supposed to be their run.
The driver cracked the whip and cried,
"Mush, you huskies, mush."
With Balto in the lead,
They ran off in a rush.

★★★★★

Balton the hero.
Lived in the ice and snow.
There was nowhere in the frozen north
That Balto could not go.
The bravest and the fastest,
He'll be forever known
As the dog who saved the people
Who lived way up in Nome.

★★★★★

Hank Niceley

They ran out in the snowy night
With snow up to their backs.
But Balto did not panic,
He got them back on track.
They crossed a frozen river
And the medicine was lost,
But the driver found it in the snow
And then they traveled on.

★★★★★

Balto saved them from cracking ice,
And through the storm they ran.
There were no lights at Safety Point,
So they ran on again.
They were cold and tired but Balto led,
And they all followed him
'Till he finished what he started,
Balto would not quit.

★★★★★

Balto the hero
Lived in the ice and snow.
There was nowhere in the frozen north
That Balto could not go.
The bravest and the fastest,
He'll be forever known
As the dog who saved the people

Who lived way up in Nome.

★★★★★

When they saw the lights of Nome,
They had run for twenty hours.
Balto was too tired to bark
But he had made it now.
Balto was a hero.
The medicine arrived.
The bravest dog had led them all
And saved the people's lives.

★★★★★

Balto the hero.
Lived in the ice and snow.
There was nowhere in the frozen north
That Balto could not go.
The bravest and the fastest,
He'll be forever known
As the dog who saved the people
Who lived way up in Nome.

A Great Natural Asset

The Mother of Scandal

Petroleum has been used in many forms for thousands of years in all parts of the world. The Bible says that Noah used "pitch" to seal cracks in the ark. (Genesis 6:14). Egyptians and Chinese used petroleum products for lubrication and fuel.

Oil was discovered in America when Edwin Drake, a retired railroad conductor, struck oil near Titusville, Pennsylvania.

The petroleum industry is a huge part of the economics and politics of the United States. Taxes on petroleum products support many government programs. Gasoline taxes build new roads and maintain existing roads. Oil companies are large buyers of products and employers of people. It would be difficult to overestimate the power of the oil industry.

When there is that much money involved, it is inevitable that greed will show its ugly face. Whoever controls the oil lands is in a position to make millions of dollars.

Oil producers who want access to the oil lands may offer financial temptations for favoring them.

As more and more oil was discovered on government land, the temptations proved to be too strong for some powerful government officials to resist.

Secrecy is the greatest ally of deceit, so those who planned and executed plans for personal profit tried to keep their "deals" secret. Sometimes their devious dealing was discovered and there was a huge public scandal. The government may be embarrassed. Powerful individuals may be ruined. Careers may be killed. Oil is a powerful asset, but it has often been the mother of scandal.

There are important decisions to be made, and soon, in regard to the energy situation in America. Shall we continue to be dependent on foreign suppliers who do not have our good in their strategies or shall we strive to, as quickly as possible to become our own energy master? This is an acute way-of-life decision and a necessary national security decision. We cannot make no decision. We have plenty of energy sources of our own. Do we have the will to use them all, now? It is not simply a matter of using what we have. We must also learn to conserve what we have. We must develop new sources to replace our heavy reliance on petroleum. Many newer cars are equipped to use flex fuel. Flex fuel is used just like pure gasoline but it is 85% ethanol, corn. It is cheaper and it is renewable.

I recently rode in a shuttle van from my hotel in Oklahoma City to the airport. The driver told me that it was running on natural gas. He could purchase natural gas for his vehicle at only a few places but it was vastly cheaper in cost. The problem of distribution of energy sources such as flex fuel and natural gas must be addressed and more vehicles must be built equipped to use them.

I have even given thought to the old Stanley Steamer. The Stanley Motor Carriage Company in Newton, Massachusetts produced steam-powered vehicles between 1902 and 1924. The Stanley Steamer had a wooden body and a boiler and burner beneath the seat. This was later placed in the front where the gasoline engine is normally located. It was fitted with safety valves. When the internal explosion engine threatened to make the Stanley Steamer obsolete, the company embarked on an advertising campaign. The slogan, "Power Correctly Generated, Power Correctly Controlled." Did not prevent the demise of the company and the car.

Although there were some drawbacks compared to the faster gasoline powered counterpart, the advantages are obvious. Water is cheaper than petroleum and steam engins emit no pollution. With all of our modern knowledge and our native ingenuity, is it possible to go back to the future with steam powered vehicles as one arrow in our quiver of solutions to our energy problem? Just think! Every home could have its rain barrels and, like manna from heaven, collect totally free fuel. Well, we went to the moon, didn't we?

If we do fill our quiver with arrows, we can have a great future as a nation. If we do not, it is very likely that we will find ourselves in a continual decline until, someday, others will be making our decisions for us. This is our country. Let's all do everything possible, even if it requires great sacrifice, to preserve it for our descendants.

Mr. Fall Caused His Own Fall

Teapot Dome

He was born in Kentucky.
His family raised him there.
He was smart and from the start,
He knew he'd go somewhere.
He became a lawyer
And soon his time would come.
Elected as a Senator,
He moved to Washington.

*****

He learned the ways of Washington
And knew the president.
Appointed to Harding's cabinet,
Temptation raised its head.
The time would come when he'd succumb.
For money he would fall.
He tried to keep it secret,
But soon 'twas known by all.

*****

Greed became his enemy
When it looked him in the face.
He walked its ground and it brought him down
And left him in disgrace.

★★★★★

A big investigation
In nineteen twenty-three
Discovered all of his misdeeds
And irregularities.
Albert Fall had persuaded
Edward Denby to transfer
Into Fall's department
Some Western oil reserves.

★★★★★

They kept it all a secret
Until nineteen twenty-three
When the Senators discovered
His greed and bribery.
One hundred thousand dollars
Was placed in Fall's two hands.
By a private oil producer
To lease these oil rich lands.

★★★★★

Easy money made in secret,
He could not resist.
So Mister Fall fell for it all
As he closed his greedy fist.

★★★★★

Another oil producer
Gave three hundred thousand more.
For the leases in Wyoming
At a place called "Teapot Dome."
The oil men would be richer
If the public never knew.
But a day of accounting
Was surely coming soon.

★★★★★

This was the biggest scandal
Of Warren Harding's time.
When his secret became public
Albert Fall had to resign.
He spent one year in prison
And his money was all gone.
All because he caused the scandal
That we know as "Teapot Dome."

★★★★★

Mister Fall caused his own fall
For his ill-gotten gain.
"Teapot Dome" will always be
Written by his name.

State of Tennessee vs. John Thomas Scopes

Little town – Big Issue

In March of 1925, the Tennessee legislature passed a law called "The Butler Act." It prohibited teaching of "any theory which denies the story of the Divine creation of man as taught in the Bible" or that "man is descended from a lower form of animal."

During the hot summer of 1925, a little town in East Tennessee found itself right in the middle of a legal, political, and religious firestorm. A young high school biology teacher named John Thomas Scopes had defied the state law and taught his students about Charles Darwin's theory of evolution. He was indicted and brought to trial. On July 10, 1925, the little courtroom was packed with news people and spectators as Judge John T. Raulston brought down the gavel to begin one of the most famous trials in American history. For eight days, Clarence Darrow (defense) and William Jennings Bryan (prosecution) fought a fierce verbal battle as the world listened in.

The Butler Act prohibited the teaching of evolution in Tennessee schools. Darwin said, "If you can take a thing like evolution and make it a crime to teach it…you may ban books and newspapers…and try to foist your own religion upon the mind of men." John Scopes said, "By respecting the other man's views and by protecting his liberties, we gain respect for our own liberties."

The law was the law, however, and John Scopes was convicted and fined one hundred dollars. He was ultimately let off on a technicality. About forty years later, the Butler Law was repealed. The trial came to be known as "The Monkey Trial." It was made famous by the drama *Inherit the Wind*, which was written by Jerome Lawrence and Robert E. Lee in the nineteen fifties, and the movie based on this drama.

I grew up and have lived most of my life in Tennessee, near the site of this trial. I have encountered some of the viewpoints on either side of this issue. I do not believe such a trial could happen today. Even though there are still some who believe that humans developed from monkeys, and there are those who believe that God created us as we are, I believe there is more civil discourse between the two viewpoints today.

Have you heard about the man who thought he could do anything God could do? He told God that and God tested him. "OK," God said, "Make me a person."

"Sure," said the man. "I can do that." He reached down to the ground and got a hand full of dirt to make a person from dust just as God had done. "The Lord God formed the man from the dust of the ground and breathed into his nostrils the breath of life, and the man became a human being." (Genesis 2:7 NIV)

As he began to form the dirt into the form of a person, God said to him, "Get your own dirt." If man evolved from a big bang, who made the matter that banged?

There are many other theories and beliefs about the origins of humanity. Religion and/or science are the basis of most.

I have encountered some who took action to try to control the thinking and teaching in the college where I spent almost four decades as a Professor. They were in the minute minority and their efforts were not successful. Free thought and discussion, whatever the viewpoint, should be guarded carefully. Disagreement is natural. Imposition of one's own viewpoint on others who do not share it is un-American. Examine your own views about the origin and nature of mankind. Be open to listen to and read about other viewpoints. Respect others as you discuss your ideas. America is a diverse country. We do not have to agree to be agreeable.

The Monkey Trial Still Lives

Their Best Known Legacy

In a little town in Tennessee
Hidden in the hills.
People went about their lives
Just doing the Lord's will
Farms and schools and churches.
Children grew up good.
Strangers stayed just long enough
For gas and southern food.

***** *****

This little town was Dayton, in the county of Rhea.
On state highway twenty-seven.
Chattanooga's down that way.
Children went to school there.
Their teacher was John Scopes.
He taught them science his way.
But the law said he must go.

***** *****

The law said what he could not teach
But he taught it anyway.
The little town of Dayton
Would never be the same.

★★★★★

Scopes needed a good lawyer,
And this teacher got the best.
A man named Clarence Darrow
Was ready for the test.
He was known throughout the country
As a friend of the oppressed.
To defend John Scopes from those legal folks
He came from the Midwest.

★★★★★

The town was filled with people
In nineteen twenty-five.
The lawyers and the newsmen
Came there from far and wide.
White shirts and black suspenders.
Each got their turn to speak.
It was so hot sometimes they got
Outside beneath the trees.

★★★★★

The law said what he could not teach
So they put the man on trial.
The little town of Dayton
Was well- known for a while.

★★★★★

William Jennings Bryan
Was the prosecutor then.
He believed the law was right.
Monkeys did not turn to men.
Darwin's evolution
Was not believed by him
That we evolved from monkeys
Was not our maker's plan.

★★★★★

The trial was for a teacher
Who taught forbidden words.
He broke the laws of Tennessee
And spoke unholy words.
Forever Dayton, Tennessee
Will be known for this one thing.
The "Monkey Trial" will always be
Their best- known legacy.

★★★★★

The law said what he could not teach,
So they convicted him.
He was fined one hundred dollars.
Then the crowds went home again.
In thirty years they changed that law
For teachers such as him.
But the town of Dayton, Tennessee
And the "Monkey Trial" still live.

Child Labor

Chained to Their Machines

For centuries, the children of many countries have been forced to work long hours at hazardous jobs. During the 1700s and 1800s, children eight and ten years old (sometimes as young as five or six) worked in mines and factories. Sometimes they were even chained to their machines and forced to work there for as long as sixteen hours. Since this deprived them of schooling, they were left with no way to rise above doing unskilled labor.

Great Britain had passed a child labor law in 1802. The law was expanded and strengthened in 1819 and 1833. In 1839, Germany enacted their own law. In America, similar laws were being passed by the states and by the federal government. In 1930, the Children's Charter of the White House Conference on Health and Protection revealed a purpose of child labor legislation.

"For every child protection against labor that stunts growth, either physical or mental, that limits education, and deprives children of the right of comradeship, of play, and of joy."

In 1936, Massachusetts passed the first state child labor law in the United States.

In 1916, US Congress passed the first federal child labor law in the United States.

In 1918, this law was declared unconstitutional by the US Supreme Court.

In 1938, the Fair Labor Standards Act stated the rules for employing minors. This time the law stood the constitutional test.

In 1950, the Mid-Century White House Conference on Children and Youth lists some aspects of child labor laws in America.

"…to include minimum age and wages, as well as hours of work, night work, protection from hazardous occupation, provision for workman's compensation."

The young boys who worked in mines and on such projects as the Erie Canal were doing hazardous work. Many were killed on the job. Many others became old and sick before they were thirty years old. The "powder monkeys" who lit the powder charges on the canal were tied to their jobs by necessity even though they were not chained to their machines.

Child labor is still acceptable in many parts of the world. Children as young as pre-teens are put to work long hours in factories making goods to be sold to us and other countries around the world. In the past, child labor has been acceptable in America. The "powder monkeys" of the Erie Canal is just one example of this. Their lives were exploited for profit. Child labor laws have almost entirely put a stop to this in America but what is our responsibility to this phenomenon in other countries?

When you purchase goods, do you ever think of the conditions under which they were produced? Were children exploited to produce the tee shirt you are wearing? What can be done to help the oppressed children who are modern day "powder monkeys"? There are efforts in this fight underway. We can join them to make companies aware of the conditions under which the products they are selling are produced. We can do our best to purchase goods which are not produced by child labor. Our country has gone through its child labor growing pains with people like the "powder monkeys". Let's be sure we do not support surrogates now.

Clinton's Ditch

A Waterway to the West

Before the era of railroads in America, there was a great need for a means of transporting goods westward from the Atlantic Ocean and the Hudson River to the Great Lakes. In 1827, the New York legislature authorized the construction of the Erie Canal. Construction began immediately. By 1925, the project was finished at a cost of seven million dollars. This was quickly recovered from tolls. By 1882, the state had taken in more than one hundred twenty million dollars.

Commerce boomed, and cities grew up all along the canal. When the railroad came, business on the canal began to dwindle. Between 1905 and 1918 the old canal was improved and modernized. Now it is called New York State Barge Canal.

The man behind the planning of the canal was Doctor Witt Clinton. Those who were opposed to it called it "Clinton's Ditch." Clinton was on the "Seneca Chief," which was the first boat to navigate the full length of the canal.

The Erie Canal is an engineering marvel. It is about five hundred miles long with all of its sections. There were eighty three locks on the original canal to raise the boats more than five hundred feet from sea level in the east to Buffalo on Lake Erie.

The high walls were cut from solid stone by hand using powder left over from the War of 1812. Since there were no child labor laws in those days, young boys were used to light the charges set deep in the cracks of the rocks. This was dangerous work. The boys were called "powder monkeys." Many of the young "Powder Monkeys" were killed on the job before they reached their thirteenth year. The company was to pay them their wages for the year when they reached thirteen. If they died early, the company profited by not having to pay out the money earmarked for the "Powder Monkey's" wages.

Along each side of the canal was a tow path for the mules that pulled the barges through the water. Each team of mules pulled for fifteen miles each day before being relieved by fresh mules. The Erie Canal was made famous by the old song, "Fifteen Miles on the Erie Canal."

The "powder monkeys" were sacrificed for progress and profit. The old song "Fifteen Miles On The Erie Canal" might be rewritten in the light of our present-day stand on child labor, as "Sacrifice on the Erie Canal". We have come a long way but we must be reminded where we came from

Hank Niceley

in order to not revert to former practices. Let this past be seen as a growing pain not to be revisited.

Powder Monkey:
If You're in Luck, the Odds You'll Buck (A song by Hank Niceley)

From the Atlantic Ocean
To Niagara and Great Lakes.
Three hundred sixty-five miles long.
Many died along the way.
They call this modern marvel
The Erie Canal.
Blasting rocks and building locks
That we're still using now.

★★★★★

I was a young lad, only twelve,
Tall and slender, too.
I came from poor beginnings,
I never went to school.
My Pa had died, my Ma was sick.
I was the oldest, too.
I had to make it on my own,
So I found a job to do.

★★★★★

They were digging out that big canal,
Working day and night.
Blasting rocks along both sides
With drills and dynamite.
They called us Powder Monkeys.
We climbed down in the cracks
To the holes made by the star drill
To light the dynamite.

★★★★★

Powder Monkey climb down slow.
Light that powder fuse your way.
Climb up fast or you won't last
To collect your hard-earned pay.
You're twelve years old, young and bold.
There's danger way down there.
If you're in luck, the odds you'll buck
And you'll see your thirteenth year.

★★★★★

I climb down in the crevices
Like a monkey on a limb.
To set afire that powder fuse
And climb back up again.
I climb up fast out of that hole
Before the fuse burns down.
If I move too slow from down below,
I will be heaven bound.

★★★★★

The company took full charge of me,
Said they'd pay me in one year.
Right on my thirteenth birthday,
If they see that I'm still here.
If that dynamite blows me away,
Before I reach that day,
There'll be one less Powder Monkey.

★★★★★

Powder Monkey climb down slow.
Light that powder fuse your way.
Climb up fast or you won't last
To collect your hard earned pay.
You're twelve years old, young and bold.
There's danger way down there.
If you're in luck, the odds you'll buck
And you'll see your thirteenth year.

★★★★★

There's a little cemetery
With rows of little stones.
With names of Powder Monkeys
Buried down below.
The dates on every tombstone
Can bring a man to tears.

Most Powder Monkeys never lived
One day past thirteen years.

★★★★★

Powder Monkey, climb down slow.
Light that powder fuse your way.
Climb up fast, or you won't last
To collect your hard owned pay.
You're twelve years old, young and bold.
There's danger way down there.
If you're in luck, the odds you'll buck
And you'll see your thirteenth year.

A Model of Modesty

Moral and Right

Paris and New York City were the centers of the art world. How could a young boy from the farmland of Iowa, so far away from these places, realize his dream of becoming an artist? He grew up in Cedar City, Iowa, but his dreams reached far beyond his home.

Like many aspiring artists of that day, Grant Wood managed to go to Europe to search for his artistic roots and inspiration. After a time back home, he again traveled to Europe. This time he discovered the medieval paintings of the Flemish and German artists. It seemed that he had found his artistic heart. He returned home with renewed determination to paint the people and places he knew so well. He painted his neighbors with a precision reminiscent of the Flemish paintings he had seen in Europe. It would not be long before the nation would recognize this midwest artist.

In 1930 Wood exhibited a small painting at the Art Institute of Chicago. They bought it and it became an icon of American art.

"American Gothic" is painted with oils on beaverboard. It is only about twenty-four by thirty inches in size. Although it appears to be a simple portrait of a Midwestern couple standing in front of their farmhouse, it is much more.

The woman is the artist's sister, Nan Wood Graham. The man is the local dentist. They stand as firmly as the orderly life they live. The man holds a pitchfork as if to say to any would intrude, "This is our way of life. Try to disturb it at your own risk."

Grant Wood had his critics who sought to marginalize his work and that of other "regionalists" as they called them. Just as Jan Vermeer had spent his artistic life painting pictures in a few rooms of his house, Grant Wood painted the people and places close to home that he knew well. To marginalize such work is to say, unless one paints about some great well-known subject, his work is inferior. The reason this painting has become one of America's best-known paintings is its honesty of spirit. It tells the truth about a way of life and the people who lived it. The house behind them is simple. The people's dress and countenance is simple. There is no attempt to show the people he knew in a way that he thought others might want them to be. He painted them the way they were. His skill at painting and his honesty of depiction combine to make this a real American masterpiece.

America has changed during the decades since this painting was first displayed. There are still many small-towns and small-town folks, but for the most part, their lives are different now. An honest depiction of such a couple would not place the woman behind the man in a secondary position. The house would probably be larger now. Instead of a pitchfork, he might be holding the keys to the large John Deere machine that he uses to pull his combine. These intervening years have been growing pains for our country. They have included wars and a great depression, but Life in America has survived the growing pains and improved. Sometimes it is good to take stock of where we are and where we came from. "American Gothic" is a big part of our country's roots preserved by a skillful and honest painter.

It became a symbol of the virtuous, honest way of life. Others may have longed for such a life. It is a mode of modesty—moral and right.

American Gothic

Grant Wood's Masterpiece (A song by Hank Niceley)

I look like a farmer.
She looks like my wife.
We live close together.
We have a good life.
I like her new apron
With rick-rack around.
It's made from a feed sack
I got for my cow.

★★★★★

I'm really her dentist,
And if you just knew
How I fixed her molars
When they were askew.
She needs some more work,
For she dips her snuff.
Her teeth are all yellow,
So her mouth is shut.

★★★★★

American Gothic,
Grant Wood's masterpiece.
These common folk heroes stand firmly at ease.
Their life of hard work
In their Iowa town
Is simple and disciplined,
Solid and sound.

★★★★★

The farmhouse behind me
Is neat and it's clean.
One pointed window
And a porch barely seen.
While I pose for this painting,
No work for a while.
To see if I'm happy,
Just look at my smile.

★★★★★

My pitchfork protects me
And my way of life.
You might just get stuck
If you bother my wife.
She stands here beside me,

But where is her mind?
That painter's my brother,
I'll bake him a pie.

★★★★★

American Gothic,
Grant Wood's masterpiece.
These common folk heroes
Stand firmly at ease.
Their life of hard work
In this Iowa town
Is simple and disciplined,
Solid and sound.

The Secret Is Out

The State's Fifth Largest City

About twenty miles northwest of Knoxville, Tennessee, the rural way of life persisted. In the beautiful foothills of the Smoky Mountains, along the rivers and among the wooded ridges, people lived much as they had done since the area was settled. The valleys were prone to flooding until the Tennessee Valley Authority began to build dams on the rivers in the 1930s. The dams provided flood control and electric power. This changed their lives somewhat, but it would be another decade before their lives would be changed forever.

The Louisville and Nashville Railroad ran right through this area. Otherwise it was an isolated valley when the Federal Government bought 30,000 acres in Anderson County and 28,000 acres in Roane County. This site was chosen because there was plenty of water and electricity there. About one thousand families had to be moved out of the area.

In February of 1943, construction started on a huge plant to produce uranium 235. In less than one year, the buildings were in operation. By 1945, there were 20,000 workers and a general population of about 50,000.

Oak Ridge remained essentially a secret city until August, 1945, when President Harry Truman announced that the atomic bomb had been produced in Oak Ridge, Tennessee. The people of the area were astounded when they heard what had been going on right in their back yard. Workers in this obscure little mountain valley had produced something which would affect the entire world for centuries to come. Today other countries might have their "secret cities" in operation now. It is hoped that those who develop their own atomic energy have good motives for its use.

Since World War II, Oak Ridge has continued to be an important research center for peaceful uses of atomic energy and other work. The Oak Ridge Associated Laboratories and the Museum of Atomic Energy are located there. The guard gates are gone now. The secret is out. Oak Ridge is now the fifth largest city in the state of Tennessee.

As a small boy, I remember driving in through the Edgemore Gate with my mother. She was a seamstress and had to go into Oak Ridge periodically to deliver some of her work to someone who lived there. We were stopped at the gate. Papers were examined and the gate opened for us to drive through. The city was covered with houses that we called "flat-tops". They were small square buildings with a flat roof that had been provided for the large workforce there in the early years. I did not know it then, but I had just entered one of the United State's war secrets. What was being developed there would soon be known by everyone in the world. It would end a war.

For more than half a century this thing has caused dissention between countries. Some believe it has saved lives. It obviously took lives when it, the atomic bomb, was dropped on two cities in Japan. The United States now has the distinction of the only nation to ever drop an atomic bomb on another country.

I often wonder if another choice might have had the same result without annihilating two whole cities and their people. Could we have dropped the bomb, as a demonstration of our power, on an uninhabited island near Japan and sunk the island? Would that have achieved a surrender and the end of the war? We can never know for sure, but the beginning of the atomic age was a definite a growing pain for us and other nations. This pain has never subsided. We must deal with it every day. The spread of these weapons of mass destruction has made it necessary to do our best to control such power. Well into the next century, most of the free world is united in an effort to keep Iran from developing their own nuclear weapon.

Being a nuclear power seems to have become the ticket to political power in the world community. People around the world are concerned that sometime soon a rogue nation or a terrorist group will come into the possession of a nuclear weapon, and use it. When seeds are sown, a harvest will appear. The United States, right or wrong, did sow the first seed of nuclear destruction in 1945. The harvest has been there to reap ever since. This is one growing pain that is still growing and still painful.

The Secret City

Turning War into Peace

World events were turbulent.
World War II continued on.
People in the government
Sought a way to make it stop.
People still were killing
And dying, ours and theirs.
Emotions high on every side,
But solutions were rare.

★★★★★

In a little mountain valley,
In the state of Tennessee,
Where little farms and farmers,
And forest used to be.
Things began to happen,
But few knew what it was.
But they knew it was important
To our nation's history.

★★★★★

Local people were evicted.
Workers came from everywhere.
Dormitories were constructed.
There was excitement in the air.
Everyone who entered,
Must be checked at city gates.
They were sworn to secrecy.
They just had to work and wait.

★★★★★

Just a few miles west of Knoxville.
Not shown on any map.
They built a "Secret City"
In only three years flat.
Seventy-five thousand people
In nineteen forty-five,
Lived and worked at Y12,
X10 and K25.

★★★★★

They called this secret city
Clinton's engineering Works.
Near the little town of Clinton
Is where the secret lurked.
When the war was over,
The secret was out.
Fuel for the first atomic bomb
Was produced in that town.

★★★★★

Now the "Secret City" is open.
The guard gates are all gone.
The people and the city,
Through the years have grown.
Today it's known throughout the world
As Oak Ridge, Tennessee.
The "Secret City" did its part
Turning war into peace.

Both Honored and Hated

Heroes on the Front Lines of History

Civil rights are prescribed by a community for its people. It may be a nation or a state or a city. These rights have varied widely throughout history in various cultures. The rights might be guaranteed by law or understood by custom.

The United States Constitution describes the civil rights guaranteed to all the citizens of the country. States and cities have passed their own civil rights laws. Among these rights are freedom of assembly, freedom of religion, freedom of speech, and the right to vote. Minority rights are protected.

The largest minority group in America is African Americans. In 1865, the thirteenth amendment abolished slavery. Three years later, former slaves were made citizens by the fourteenth amendment. In the southern states transportation, restaurants, water fountains, and schools were segregated on a "separate-but-equal" rule. This rule was broken in 1954 by the Brown vs. Board of Education of Topeka case. The Supreme Court ruled that segregation was not constitutional. In 1957, the Civil Rights Act was passed.

During the next two decades the civil rights movement was invigorated by a few brave leaders. In 1955, Rosa Parks refused to give up her seat on a city bus to a white person. This protest grew into a larger movement. A Baptist minister named Martin Luther King led marches and rallies on behalf of equality for every person. In his most famous speech in Washington, DC, King said that his dream for America was that each person would be judged on the content of their character instead of the color of their skin.

In 1968, King was in Memphis to support striking sanitary workers. Although his method was non-violence, violence seemed to find him. As he stood on his motel balcony, he was killed by the bullet of a hidden rifleman.

Many others were active in the civil rights movement, but these two pioneer leaders risked their lives out front. They were both honored and hated, but they were brave heroes on the front lines of history.

I remember the "White" and" "Colored" water fountains. I remember hearing the word "nigger" used often by white people as I grew up. I remember having only one black family living anywhere near me. One of their boys and I carried morning newspapers together. I liked him and envied him. I carried papers on my bicycle. He had a real pony.

I remember the time, in college, that I brought some black people to campus in my car to participate in a race relations symposium. We went into the cafeteria to eat before the meeting. They were refused service. I had to eat with them in a side room closed off from the other students. This was not only racism at its worst but it was selective racism. As the local Black people were forced to eat in the side room away from the other students, or not eat there, there were other blacks eating out in the dining hall. They were from Africa, brought to the College by Missionaries to Africa. There seemed to be some real difference between the two kinds of Blacks to the college. I am thankful to say that this attitude and practice has been long gone for many years.

I remember Selma, Alabama. I remember the march in Montgomery. I remember Washington D.C. and Martin Luther King's great speech, "I Have A Dream". I remember when he was killed in Memphis. I remember the variety of comments by people I knew and those I didn't know. Some expressed sorrow at King's death. Some expressed joy that the leader of the people they hated was dead. Years later, I remember what one of the men who is suspected of being involved in the murder of Medgar Edgars, a civil rights activist at that time, said. When asked if he murdered Mr. Edgars, he replied with satisfaction in his voice, "No. but he shore is dead, ain't he." I also remember some major leaders in the south who had stood for segregation forever, recanting and changing their beliefs and actions.

I have lived through some powerful growing pains for our country. Those pains are not nearly as strong as they were back then, but they can still be felt. We must continue to treat this old wound with love and fairness and respect for all others until we are free of it.

Up Front for All the Rest

Rosa and Martin (A Song by Hank Niceley)

Step right up, but walk right by.
Don't sit down by me.
This place beside me is not for you,
Even though this seat is free.
Go to the back where you belong,
Or we'll put you in jail.
Your skin is not like my skin.
And my skin will prevail.

★★★★★

She had heard these words before,
But today she had enough.
Rosa Parks sat down there anyway,
On that bus—up in the front.
Someone white asked to sit there
In the seat where Rosa sat.
"Go to the back. I'm white, you're black.
Don't think of coming back."

★★★★★

Rosa was a hero
To those who were oppressed.
She rode the bus to freedom,
Up front like all the rest.

★★★★★

He was a Baptist minister,
Who fought for equal rights.
Wanting to see equality
For every black and white.
He took a stand for every man,
Always in a peaceful way.
Martin made a difference.
But a high price he would pay.

★★★★★

Stabbed in New York City.
In Chicago he was stoned.
His home in Alabama,
By his enemies was bombed.
In April, nineteen sixty-eight in Memphis,
Tennessee,
Someone shot and killed him
On his motel balcony.

★★★★★

Martin was a hero
To those who were oppressed.
He marched and spoke for freedom
Up front of all the rest.

★★★★★

Many dreamed of freedom,
Not knowing what to do.
But on that bus Rosa Parks
Started something new.
Walking in her footsteps,
Martin Luther King
Led the way to a brand new day,
When he said, "I have a dream."

★★★★★

Many dreamed of freedom
But their dream remained a dream.
Very few, like these two,
Risked losing everything.
They sang the song of freedom.
"We Shall Overcome".
Their dream is coming true today,
But there is more to come.

★★★★★

Hank Niceley

Everybody needs their heroes
To fight for the oppressed.
Who dream aloud and stand their ground,
Up front for all the rest.

★★★★★

Rosa Parks and M.L. King
Were soldiers in a war.
Their weapon was non-violence.
Courage was their uniform.
Their courage is a beacon
To all who have a dream.
Their names will live forever
In our nation's history.

★★★★★

They were courageous heroes
To those who were oppressed.
They risked their lives for freedom,
Up front for all the rest.

Have you ever been "the only one"? I have been in some places in the world where I was the only one who spoke English. There was some fear involved. How do I communicate what I need? How do I know what they are saying and feeling about me? What if you were in a place where you were certain that the people around you hated you and would even kill you if possible. There certainly would be fear involved there. But would you have the courage to stand your ground in a peaceful way and hope you would not be harmed? Peter was in a similar situation when Jesus was taken prisoner in Jerusalem. After swearing that he would not deny him, Peter denied Jesus three times in order to save himself. (Matthew 26:69-75.) The crowds there were hostile to Jesus and anyone who was associated with him. They could have killed Peter if he had admitted that he knew Jesus. He lacked the courage to admit his association with Jesus.

A Christian man in Iran has recently been charged and threatened with death for converting to Christianity and not being willing to denounce his conversion from Islam. By the time this book is published, that man will likely have been assasinated for his religious beliefs.

Martin Luther King and Rosa Parks, and other African Americans such as those who entered white schools in Birmingham, Alabama, Clinton, Tennessee, and Little Rock, Arkansas were brave enough to be "the only one." What do you believe for which you would be willing to be "the only one"?

Watergate: The Downfall of a President

"I am not a crook." These words might be expected from someone who is accused of a crime. He might be innocent, or he might want to convince everyone of his innocence to avoid punishment.

But this was not being said by any common criminal. It was the president of the United States, Richard Nixon. It was 1972, and the country was in the midst of an election for president. In order to get special information about the other side, it was decided to break into and wiretap the Watergate apartment that was serving as the headquarters of the opposite political party. The burglars were caught in the act. What followed was a national upheaval.

It began with the arrest of five men. The United States Senate appointed a Watergate Committee to investigate the incident. Eventually, their hearings were televised. The entire country was glued to their television sets as the names of conspirators Dean, Ehrlichman, Haldeman, Hunt, and Liddy became household names.

The investigation revealed that the president had recorded conversations in the oval office between himself and the conspirators. After court battles that led all the way to the United States Supreme Court, on July 30, 1974, the recordings were handed over to the committee. The recording revealed that the president was directly implicated in trying to cover up the break-in.

On March 1, 1974, the grand jury indicted seven of the president's former aides. Colson, Haldeman, Ehrlichman, Mitchell, Strachan, Mardian, and Parkinson became known as the "Watergate Seven."

President Nixon was facing sure impeachment. On August 9, 1974, he resigned the presidency. After his resignation, the Watergate Committee dropped impeachment proceedings against him. Vice President Gerald Ford succeeded Nixon.

On September 8, 1974, President Ford issued an unconditional pardon of Nixon. He said in his televised announcement of the pardon that he felt that the pardon was "in the best interest of the country." He called the episode in our nation's history "an American tragedy in which we all have played a part."

Nixon insisted that he was innocent until his death in 1994. Ford wrote about his decision to pardon Nixon in his autobiography *A Time to Heal*.

The prediction attributed to Secretary of State Henry Kissinger that Watergate would be relegated to a "minor footnote" did not seem to hold true. The Watergate scandal that caused the downfall of a president has left a lasting impression in the history of our nation. Many scandals since then have been labeled with the suffix "gate."

The Watergate scandal was such a big event in the consciousness of our nation that the last part of the word, "gate", has become a symbol of deception and scandal in many situations since. I remember watching our president Nixon looking us all in the eye on television and saying, "I am not a crook." I also remember hearing the evidence against him and his men in the Watergate hearings. Then I remember his resignation. This was an embarrassing and sad time in America. Our own President had deceived us and lied about it. This was a growing pain which spawned others. Sadly, deception by our leaders has continued. Every year there are accusations and some convictions for unethical and unlawful actions by elected officials. If we do not cure our growing pains we are forced to endure them again and again.

We have the right to expect good from our elected officials, but not perfection. Everyone has their flaws, even the President of the United States of America. Sometimes the isolation of the office might give the president the feeling that he is invincible, that he can do anything. He may come to believe that the law is not for him. Our form of government has checks and balances which keep any one facet of the government from going too far. There are boundaries even for those in the highest office. Richard Nixon found this out the hard way. There are no excuses for the actors in the Watergate scandal, but we should remember the good they might have done and be careful who we elect in the future. And remember in your judging, "Let he who is without sin cast the first stone.". (John 8:7) I guess there are times when we must judge others, but we should temper our judgment with forgiveness and determination to walk the better path.

A Skyscraper was the Symbol:
Grief and Heroism was the Reality

As the big cities grew, land became expensive. Buildings had spread out horizontally until someone had the idea to spread vertically. More floor space could be achieved without having to purchase more expensive land. This was a uniquely American idea at the time, but soon the skyline of almost every large city in the world would be changed.

Chicago was the birthplace of the skyscraper. The first tall building was designed by William Le Baron Jenney. The Home Insurance building was constructed in 1879 and torn down in 1931. It was only ten stories tall, but it started a revolution in urban architecture.

With the taller buildings came a need to raise people to the upper floors. In the 1850s, Elisha Otis invented his "safety lift," now called the elevator. Steel allowed builders to construct taller buildings rather than with masonry. In 1931, the 1,250 foot tall Empire State Building was the tallest building in the world. It was inevitable that builders would build taller and taller structures. Frank Lloyd Wright even proposed a mile-high skyscraper for Chicago. In 1973, the 110 story World Trade Center Towers were built in New York City. They quickly became a recognizable symbol of the New York City skyline. They were located in the financial district of lower Manhattan. For almost three decades, this city within a city was a very busy place. Every morning, the elevators were filled with people going to their office for another normal day of work.

Times were changing. Unknown to those who worked in the two towers and everyone else, tragedy was about to visit. On September 11, 2001, just before nine o'clock in the morning, the world woke up to the emotional voices of news reporters describing terrible events unfolding in New York City. The two towers had been deliberately struck by two commercial airplanes commandeered by terrorists. There was terror in the air and terror on the streets. There were incredible acts of heroism. The city, the nation, and the world were changed forever. The worst and the best of humankind was among us during those terrible times. A skyscraper was the symbol, but grief and heroism were the reality of that day.

The skyscraper was born in America. It symbolized the country to the world. Those who desire to harm America decided to strike at this symbol of economic power. The American spirit was stunned at such an act of cowardice and hatred on the eleventh of September. But as always, the people first responded by helping others. Then the anger set in, aimed at Osama Ben Laden who had been deemed responsible for the evil deed. The country vowed to find him and make him pay. It took more than a decade to find him. Finally, he was discovered and killed.

Hank Niceley

At times now it seems that we have begun to forget how we felt when the twin towers were toppled in a ball of fire. A lapse of memory is a luxury we cannot afford. It is not pleasant living in a world of hostility toward you, but it is the only world we have. We must be vigilant of those who hate us. My Christian faith teaches me to love my enemies. Jesus said, "You have heard that it was said, 'Love your neighbor and hate your enemy.' But I tell you: Love your enemies and pray for those who persecute you ..." (Matthew 5:43-44). We are even told that if our enemy is hungry feed him. "If your enemy is hungry, feed him; if he is thirsty, give him something to drink." (Romans 12:20). This is not easy to do. In fact it seems almost impossible in the world climate today. But I believe we should try. Loving our enemy might take the form of praying for him or coming to the aid of the people of his country in a natural disaster. But self defense is an honorable response to the hostility of the times. We must make tough decisions nowadays. Pray for our leaders' wisdom.

We will rebuild our skyscrapers. We will protect ourselves and our way of life to the best of our ability. We will remain strong so we will have the ability to protect ourselves. The skyscraper is a symbol of growth. We endured another growing pain on September eleven. We will continue to rebuild. We will defend our way of life. We will survive. The big question for us is Will we survive with our moral compass intact?

Two Towers

Evil Came but Love Did Reign

A few white clouds to decorate
A bright blue autumn sky.
The leaves were turning color.
The sun was shining bright.
The people in the city
Were going on their way.
Everything was ordinary
Just another city day.

★★★★★

Two towers reaching skyward,
Taller than the rest.
Mothers, fathers, sons, and daughters
Sitting at their desks.
A normal day of commerce.
A normal way of life
Was about to change forever
In this city in the sky.

★★★★★

Hank Niceley

His voice was filled with unbelief,
Telling what he saw and heard.
Pictures on the TV screen
Confirming every word.
There was terror on the city streets
And terror in the sky.
Two towers in destruction,
With screams, and smoke, and fire.

★★★★★

Was this some horror movie we were watching in our homes?
Could we still be dreaming? If we woke, would it all be gone?
Will someone say, "We're sorry.
It was all a big mistake?"
Just an ordinary error
On an ordinary day.

★★★★★

Then one more time we saw it
Right before our eyes
It looked just like an airplane,
But it was hatred in disguise.
Two towers was its target.
Destruction was its plan.
Precious lives in every window
Would not be seen again.

*****

Quick last good-byes on cell phones
To loved ones safe at home.
Acts of heroism
In the face of death were done.
People helping people
They did not even know.
Hatred flew, but love did, too
As it recognized its foe.

*****

We were all in those two towers
When evil came to call.
Evil's greatest enemy
Is love, and love stood tall.
Tragedy birthed bravery
Thorns revealed the flowers.
The day that hate came calling,
We were all in those two towers.

*****

Time will soften memory.
Lessons will be learned
Evil will be conquered.
Nations will be turned.
Until the final victory,

This legacy is ours.
Evil came, but love did reign
One day at those two towers.
The eleventh of September
Burned in our memory.
A growing pain to remember
Freedom is not free.

Freedom Is not Free: A Heavy Price Has Been Paid

One must crawl before one can walk. This is also true of nations. The founders of this nation had to endure hardship and danger as they were building a new nation, "conceived in liberty and dedicated to the proposition that all men are created equal." This ideal has been and still is our enduring hope.

There have been moments of brilliance along the way. There have also been times of sorrow and shame. There were wars to be fought. First came the Revolutionary War (1775-1783) followed by the War of 1812. The Civil War (1862-1865) tested our country. The century was finished out with the Spanish-American War in 1898. The twentieth Century saw more wars. It started with World War I (1914-1918) followed by World War II (1941-1945). Then came the Korean War (1950-1953), the Viet Nam War and the Middle Eastern Wars.

Is this enough growing pains for you? I hope the growing pains are learning moments and that the twenty first century will be much more war-free. Remember that after World War II the United States spent much effort and treasure to rebuild the countries we had just defeated. The old adage, "To the victor go the spoils" had been the rule

Hank Niceley

throughout most of human history. America was a shining light upon a hill when it defied this old rule and spent its fortune to rebuilt the lands of our former enemies. We have reversed the words of Theodore Roosevelt who said "Walk softly and carry a big stick." We had carried and used our big stick during WW II. After the war, we walked softly. Is this loving our enemies?

A heavy price has been paid for our liberties. Those who died in battle paid their price. Those who stayed home and bore the loss of loved ones paid their price. The nation crawled, then walked, then ran. Sometimes growing pains were severe, but the nation has endured and sometimes she has shown her loving face.

As a child, things we need are just there for us. We do not have to earn them. We do not have to pay for them. They are just there. We have food. We have a comfortable place to sleep. We have clothing. We have parents. We give very little thought to the source of all these things until one day something is missing. War requires sacrifices by those who go and those who stay. A little boy of four cannot understand the reasons for war. He just knows his dad is gone and he misses him. When he learns that his dad has been killed in action, he must grow up fast. The little boy remembers his dad's last words to him just before he left. "Take care of Mama, son. It's your turn now."

As we read and think about the growing pains of our country and the people who lived through those times, we should be aware that it's our turn now.

It's Your Turn Now

(A song included on the CD "With Roots In God")

I was only four years old
In the front yard with my dad.
When he told me he would have to go
To war, and I was sad.
Before he left he told me
Things to do, and how.
He said, "Take care of Mama, son,
It's your turn now."

★★★★★

We ate together every night
And Mom would cook the meal.
No frozen dinners at our house.
Everything was real.
When we all were seated,
We thanked God as we bowed.
We took our turn with prayers we learned
When Dad said, "It's your turn now."

★★★★★

I did not understand back then.
Now I know he had to go,
Because he loved his family
And he loved his family so.
Now I'm a man like he was then
And I try to make him proud.
When I raised my hand and took my stand
I heard him say, "It's your turn now.

★★★★★

Dad was killed in action.
They shipped his body home
I remember at his funeral
Not believing that he's gone.
Now I'm a man like he was then
And I try to make him proud.
I still hear him say to this very day,
"Son, it's your turn now."

★★★★★

I have walked among white crosses
Of those who gave their all.
They sacrificed their young lives.
For their country, they stood tall.
As I walk here, through quiet tears,

I can hear their voices shout.
From a loving heart, we did our part.
Sons and daughters, it's your turn now.

★★★★★

There are those who would harm us,
And destroy our way of life.
We must always keep our guard up.
Keep our vigil through the night.
Blood has bought our freedom,
But our nation never bowed.
A chorus of our heroes sings,
"We're gone. It's your turn now."

★★★★★

They pledged allegiance to the flag
And went away to war.
One nation under God to guide
Our ship of state to shore.
Our children and their children
Look to us to show them how.
Will America survive while we're alive?
It's our call. It's our turn now.

The focus was on the flag-draped coffin in the front and the Marines in full dress uniforms who were about to carry it out of the church. Tears were flowing.

"He was just a boy." One whispered.

"He's a hero," said another.

The marines folded the flag in a neat triangle according to regulation and gave it to a young woman in the front row. She took it and held it close to her heart. The young woman was crying. All the talk had been about the sacrifice of the soldier. She had paid a great price too. Her husband was dead. Their newborn son would never know his dad. As she stood holding the flag near to her heart, she thought, "He gave all, we can do no less".

We Can Do No Less

(A song included on the CD "With Roots In God")

Tears had dried from her grieving eyes,
But her inner pain was strong.
They said he died a hero,
But now she was alone.
Her baby would be born today,
And she would do her best,
To accept her plight and raise him right.
God would do the rest.

★★★★★

A picture on her mantle
Of a man in uniform,
Looked like her son, forever young.
She promised him once more,
To raise the one who is their son,
She'd do her very best.
The flag would fly in their front yard sky.
She could do no less.

*****

He grew up in a southern town.
Finished high school just this year.
As long as he remembered,
Our flag had flown right here.
His dad had fought for freedom
And his love for this land.
For the promise of America
He would take his stand.

*****

"I promise to be brave and strong,
And faithful to this land.
I'll fight against all enemies
At home and foreign lands.
I'll defend this flag and freedom
I'll do my very best."
For the land his dad had died for,
He could do no less.

*****

I felt the blast and saw the fire,
And heard a soldier shout.
With the first word from his mouth,
I knew that he was from the south.
He was wounded from the impact.

He said he could not see.
Just one more yard to the left,
And it would have been me.

★★★★★

In that darkness, after midnight,
He said he saw a light.
I think he saw god calling him
On that battlefield that night.
He made me promise to be brave.
"Tell mom I did my best.
To defend the flag of freedom"
He could do no less.

★★★★★

Now there are two pictures there,
On her mantle side by side.
Two flags are folded neatly.
One flag still flies outside.
They paid a price, but so did she,
For the freedom that we see.
The promise of America
Was bought by such as these.

★★★★★

Hank Niceley

The promise of America
Is still alive today,
Because of many heroes
Who took their stand one day.
To those who came before us,
We owe a might debt.
We promise now to make them proud.
We can do no less.

"Greater love has no man than this, that he lay down his life for his friends" (John 15:13, NIV).

The United States of America is a wonderful country to call home. I am proud of her generosity and her ingenuity. I applaud her desire to help others. I love her promise of equality for everyone. These are great qualities, but America is not perfect. There have been some major mistakes as she has endured her growing pains. But to improve one must have a standard or ideal as a goal. We must always be vigilant of dropping away from our ideals. We must be mindful of efforts to draw closer to them. We are still a work in progress. Professionals and laborers, immigrants and native born citizens, rich and poor, and old and young are all of equal value according to the ideal of America.

The Ideal of America

(A song included in the CD " With Roots In God")

His hair was white. His skin was black.
He wore a three-piece suit.
Her hair was red. Her skin was white.
Her clothes were tattered too.
He stopped to help her on the street
Where she slept out in the rain.
When one stoops to help another, then
We are all the same.

★★★★★

He went to the synagogue.
She went to church to pray.
Another worshipped in a mosque,
And another stayed away.
But when we all stand side by side
In unison to say,
"I pledge allegiance to the flag."
We are all the same.

★★★★★

Different faces. Different races.
Different clothes and different names
The ideal of America,
Where everyone's the same.

★★★★★

He was dressed in overalls,
White socks and working shoes.
She wore silk she bought in stores
Along Fifth Avenue.
Side by side with American pride,
They fought with others brave.
When they wore that uniform,
They were all the same.

★★★★★

She spoke with an accent.
His was a southern drawl.
Both sang in the choir
At the local civic hall.
When they sang about "Old Glory,"
And their country strong and brave
Their voices blended perfectly.

They were all the same.

★★★★★

Different faces. Different races.
Different clothes and different names
The ideal of America,
Where everyone's the same.

★★★★★

She worked in a city office.
He worked in a mountain mine.
They stood in line, side by side,
When it was voting time.
Their time of truth in that voting booth
Did not require their name.
Once inside they chose their side,
There everyone's the same.

★★★★★

From the coal mines or the city,
Whether church or synagogue,
Male or female, black or white.
No matter where you're from.
Foreign accent or Southern drawl.
Whatever is your name.
It's the ideal of America,

Where everyone's the same.

★★★★★

Different faces. Different races.
Different clothes and different names
The ideal of America,
Where everyone's the same.

Nowadays, one does not have to travel overseas to experience the horrors of war. Television has changed everything. Reporters are embedded with the troops. Cameramen risk their lives to send pictures of warfare back to be broadcasted for all to see. War can be seen up close from one's recliner as one eats a snack and has a drink. We have seen it so much now that we may have become callous to the human suffering. Many graphic depictions of battle have been included in war movies. People flock to theatres to see them. As we sit and watch the victims of battle, Tsunami, or cyclone, it would be well for us to reflect on our responsibility toward the victims as they are suffering. Are we in some part responsible for their suffering? What can we do to alleviate their pain? What can we learn from past mistakes as we watch the scene from our place of comfort?

From My Place of Comfort

(A Song by Hank Niceley)

Born in peace and comfort,
My table is filled.
I grew up loved and sheltered
From life's fears and ills.
I am thankful daily
For God's boundless love.
Only by His mercy
Is my life so good.

*****

From my place of comfort,
I see others there.
With their tables empty,
Living in despair.
'Midst a storm of conflict,
Filled with hate and pain.
They can see no comfort,
In their life again.

*****

We are all one of God's children.
He loves us all the same.
But one child lives in luxury,
While one child lives in pain.
"Blessed is the peacemaker."
"…You have done it unto me."
He has no hands but our hands
To heal God's family.

★★★★★

Somewhere a child is hungry
With no one there to care.
He has felt the winds of terror
Take his family from him there.
On her bed of rocky rubble
She shivers all alone.
What did he do to deserve this?
Who will she blame for it all?

★★★★★

Somewhere a mother's crying
As she holds her dying son.
Disease has taken many
From her village, one by one.
With the desert sun above her
She sits there all alone.

What did she do to deserve this?
Who will she blame for it all?

★★★★★

I am thankful for your mercy
And I love America.
But there are many others
Who need our help and love.
For those whose needs are greatest,
Let my hands do your will
Take me from my place of comfort.
Some other's need to fill.

★★★★★

I was born in peace and comfort,
And I love America.
This land is blessed with plenty,
By the loving God above.
To us, much has been given.
Give us loving eyes to see.
Take us from our place of comfort,
To heal god's family.

America is a beautiful country. The Smoky Mountains
have a beauty that is different from the Rockies. The desert
and the Badlands of the Southwest have their own special
beauty. The many rivers and lakes draw us to them. The

beauty of America is not limited to her natural beauty. We are a country of givers. We give lives and treasure wherever it is needed. In natural disasters, America is usually first to show up with aid. America is the land, but most of all, it is the people. America the beautiful, this is my America.

This Is My America

(A song included I on the CD, "With Roots In God")

This is my America.
This is my homeland
From the Smoky Mountain beauty
To the western desert sand.
The rivers and the oceans
The plains with harvest rich
Under God, this is America,
And I know God gave us this.

★★★★★

America. America.
Your beauty's unsurpassed.
And if you're blessed to be the best,
Under God, this land will last.

★★★★★

This is my America.

Hank Niceley

This is my homeland.
Remember those who sacrificed
For the freedoms that we have.
We follow in their footsteps.
Our mission's worth the risk.
Under God, this is America,
And I know God gave us this.

★★★★★

America. America.
Your strength is not your own.
You were given might to use for right.
Under God, you will go on.

★★★★★

This is my America.
This is my homeland.
May we always be a beacon
And extend a helping hand.
May we all be freedom's warriors.
Never quit and never miss.
Under God, this is America.
And I know God gave us this.

★★★★★

American. America.

May freedom always stand.
A light you'll be for all to see
Under God, this is my land.

★★★★★

America. America.
Stand up for what is right.
Be sure and proud, and say out loud.
Under God, this land is mine.

Times were turbulent in the United States during the 1960s. African Americans had had enough of segregation and being treated as they had been by the whites. A leader among them emerged. Martin Luther King, a preacher from the South traveled all around the country leading other blacks in freedom demonstrations. He stood on the steps of the Lincoln Memorial in Washington D.C. and delivered a powerful speech that described the dreams of the blacks and many of the white in America. The following song was inspired by his speech, "I Have A Dream".

I Have a Dream

(A song included on the CD "With Roots In God")

I have a dream, a dream of love.
Where freedom rings for everyone.
Where sons of slaves and owners too,
Will live in brotherhood and truth.
Where we shall see beyond our sight
And there will be no black and white.
And freedom's bell will ring aloud
In tune with God in every town.

★★★★★

I have a dream, a dream of love.
Where everybody will be judged,
Not by the color of their skin
But by the character within.
Where little hands of black and white
Will hold each other in God's light.
Without a thought of us and them.

Where each is God's most precious gem.

★★★★★

I have a dream, a dream of love.
Where what has been is not enough.
Where vision clears and hearts do change,
And God's own way will be sustained.
Where every valley will be raised,
And every mountain be made low.
The glory of the Lord will be
Revealed in real equality.

★★★★★

I have a dream, a dream of love
Where freedom rings for everyone
In tune with God's own dream for us.
"As I have loved, so you must love."

★★★★★

I have a dream, a dream of love.

The Dream Continues

Growing pains are expected and even necessary. The aged wood of a fine violin offers beautiful tones, but during its aging process, the strings had to be tightened and loosened many times. Sometimes a string might break, or the bow might have to be restrung. These were like growing pains that would help it become a wonderful instrument that would produce beautiful music.

The United States of America was like a fine instrument when it was founded. Its constitution was made of good wood. It had great potential. It could not play itself. It needed master musicians with the dedication to persevere in order to fulfill its potential.

Sometimes it was picked up by lesser musicians and misused. Sometimes outside forces threatened its purity and existence. The instrument has survived all of the growing pains. What it will have to survive in the future is unknown, but with dedication to the founding principles and firm reliance on our creator, our country shall become an even more beautiful creation and force for good.

One line in the song "America the Beautiful" states, "And crown thy *good* with brotherhood." May we endure any further growing pains which might come our way and remain faithful to our moral compass. May we always strive for good. May we always be a beacon of hope. May we always be a beautifully aged instrument playing beautiful music for all who listen to hear. May we teach others by example how to play the beautiful instrument for themselves. May our dreams for this country never become a nightmare. With God's help and our love, we will survive and flourish. The dream continues.